GRIEF
LIFE

Written by Bestselling Author

Diana Register

Crazy Ink
www.crazyink.org
Formatting by Crazy Ink
Edits by Melissa Day

Grief Life/Diana Register.—1st ed.

As always, for Chad

Acknowledgements

Stephen, Savanna, Shane and Kaitlyn, you all have my heart and you know you had his. I am so proud of all of you.

My mom, for understanding what grief is and showing me how to survive.

Trina Rogers, for introducing me to what "grief life" means. #lovetohannah www.bdsra.org

My Whipple Warrior Family who understands my true grief.

My amazing friends for always standing by me and loving me through it.

To the City of Caldwell and the City of Nampa police departments for always honoring this great man of mine.

To my friends on social media near and far – I don't care if we have never met. You're my family.

For Eliza and www.lovewhatmatters.com,

for giving me a chance.

To the random people who reach out.

And to Scott – words fail me at times. Thank you for walking this crazy road with me. Thank you for wanting to hear the stories. Thank you for understanding my quirks. Thank you for loving the broken me.

Foreword

I met Diana through Facebook's Whipple Surgery Survivor's Group. Her husband had just been diagnosed with pancreatic cancer and been recommended for Whipple surgery, whereas I had just gotten out of the hospital after my own Whipple. I was diagnosed with pancreatic cancer in 2014.

I was drawn to Diana's posts and questions for several reasons – reasons that are reflected here in *Grief Life*. The first was her no-holds-barred authenticity. Diana tells it like it is and doesn't hold anything back. The second was her enduring love for her husband Chad. That love was expressed in her every word, clear and compelling. And third was her fear. Pancreatic cancer is a deadly disease and the Whipple is no guarantee of a happy outcome, as Diana's story, and my own, makes all too real. There are very few happy endings after a diagnosis of pancreatic cancer, and Diana's posts made it clear that she was afraid of losing her husband.

Because I was drawn to Diana's posts, I gave her the best, most clear and compelling answers I could. And we came to respect each other, then to appreciate each other, then to love each other.

Grief Life is not a story about how to get past your sorrow over losing a loved one. You can never truly get past it. It's not a story of triumphing over your sadness, because the sadness is always there. *Grief Life* is a story about transcending grief through embracing it, allowing it to occupy its proper place in your life without letting it break you or define you. The book is full of practical advice and emotional validation, delivered with humor, compassion, and the same sort of no-holds-barred reality that is the hallmark of Diana's writing.

As I write this, I am battling a recurrence of my pancreatic cancer. I am Stage 4 now, with no chance of winning my battle with this demon. My life span is measured in months, at best. But *Grief Life* has taught me many things that, as the dying spouse, I needed to know. Mainly, it has taught me that my family will be all right after I have left them – because I never truly leave them if they embrace what Diana is teaching in this book.

I encourage anyone who has suffered a loss (and as Diana points out, everyone has suffered a loss at some point) to read and embrace *Grief Life*.

-   Jim Hart
Raleigh-Durham Affiliate Chair
Pancreatic Cancer Action Network

Prologue

"Grief is like the ocean; it comes in waves, ebbing and flowing. Sometimes the water is calm, and sometimes it is overwhelming. All we can do is learn to swim." Vicki Harrison

My husband, Chad, died June 24, 2016. Since then, I have been trying to figure out what to do with my grief. How to process it. How to understand it. How to live with it. It's not been an easy road, but it's the road I am on, and the one I have to accept. I assume if you're reading this you have experienced a loss in your life and are grieving and trying to make sense of it much like the rest of us are.

During my healing process, I found it cathartic to write. I started journaling my grief in a series of Facebook posts and, eventually, began writing a weekly grief-type column for the website, www.lovewhatmatters.com . It was the outlet that I needed. It helped me decipher things. It helped me put what I was feeling into words and gave me the chance to get all the toxins out, so to speak. It was a release. For others, it might be exercise or a hobby or work or kids or anything that keeps them occupied, but for me, it's writing. But what I got from it was so much more than just a place to write. I got the opportunity to get to know and bond with a community of people who were feeling the same way I was. They understood. They "got it". They identified with it. And it made me realize that I am not alone.

Somewhere along the line I decided that I needed to write a book about my story, my grief and my healing process. I am so lucky that I have heard from so many people across the world who have told me their stories, but I am indebted to hear from the people who have written to me to tell me that my story has helped them. When I started receiving those, I just knew I had to write this. But, as much as I knew I needed to do this, I have struggled with how to do it. I am not a celebrity. I am not a psychologist. I am just some girl in Idaho who has lost her husband and chosen to be vocal about how awful that is. I want to write the story and give some advice but sometimes, I am not even sure I know what to do. Sometimes, I am still lost. Sometimes, I am still sitting in this weird fog and can't get out. Sometimes, I am totally confused and, sometimes, I am still angry. I questioned myself about whether or not I even had the "right" to put this all into words, but after reading some of the responses from my articles, I have realized that really, what people want to know is that they're not alone. Sure, people want to know what to do in grief. Sure, people want to know how to get through it. But what they really want is to know that somebody else knows what this feels like. They want to know that somebody else has felt a great big huge loss and they're surviving it. Yes, they want to know that you can do this without a million dollars in the bank or a following of a million people on Instagram. Yes, they want to believe that if some girl in Idaho can do it, then they can do it too.

Because that's the truth. You can, and you will, survive your grief. And, you will learn how to let it walk alongside of you as you carry on in your life.

I have been struggling with how to present this to you. I have had several different ideas on what this book would entail, and how I would give it to you. The more I think about it, the more confusing it becomes and then I overthink it and it becomes overwhelming. So, what I have decided is to just write. Just open my heart and write.

I made a commitment to myself after Chad died to be as raw, open and honest as I could be. There is no sugar coating this. There is no easy answer. There is no right or wrong way to grieve. But, it is my greatest hope that after you read this that you find some peace. That after you read this, you know you are not alone.

My husband was buried in a mausoleum. There is this tiny space between his headstone and his casket. It is barely big enough to fit anything in there, but it is big enough to fit pieces of paper if you fold them small enough. So, I write notes to him and leave them. Nobody can get to them. It's like my own personal mailbox to heaven. I hope he knows they are there. And I hope I express myself well enough. They are usually tear stained and full of babble, but I don't care, and I don't think he minds. But, in doing that, it dawned on me that sometimes I express myself best when I am writing to him. I want to share some of those with you, along with the rest of my story.

So, here goes…

Dear Chad

"When you left me, all my written lyrics become half-finished love poems, and love letters, a string of incoherent words without melody, without sound, but always with you. Love, it was always written for you." Cynthia Go

Dear Chad,

You will never believe how much has changed since you died, and how much has not. It's been almost two years and I'm still not sure I fully believe it. I still look for you in crowds. I still yearn to see your crooked, silly grin. When the back door opens, I still wonder if it's you who will come around the corner and tell me that you're home. I still half expect to open the garage door and see you sitting there playing the guitar and drinking a beer or hanging out with one of your friends playing pool. I still ache to come home at the end of a long day and tell you what happened, and have you understand.

After all, you knew everything. You knew every story; every memory and you knew exactly how to put me at ease. You knew how to fix it.

The kids are growing up. Savanna made it to USC, which is no big surprise. With a full scholarship, nonetheless. Stephen and Shane are still in the Navy and thriving. They have goals. Goals you helped them set. Did you know you're a grandpa? Your grandson was born the day before your birthday and he is beautiful. He is a sturdy little guy, just like you, and he is perfect. Stephen is a dad. Yes, Stephen is a dad. You would be pleased. Because, even though you are not here, they are living your legend. The values and morals you imparted to them are still there. They are still using them in their daily lives. And because of that, you will always, always be alive. For every generation to come, somebody will learn from the example you set as your children carry on your legacy.

Kaitlyn is a sophomore in high school. *A sophomore, Chad.* She was thirteen when you left us, and since then she's grown four inches in height and in her hair. You would be shocked, and probably horrified at how beautiful she is. I mean, she's really, really pretty. I know all parents say that, but it would floor you to see what she looks like now. She actually brushes her hair. She puts on some make-up, and contrary to what you thought, she does actually know where her socks are now. She's still sweet. I mean, some days, she drives me crazy. There's plenty of drama. But she's a teenager and your words keep ringing in my ears, "*just let her go through it, she will be ok*". That's what you would tell me. So, even on the days when I am at my wits end, I think about that. I think about how you would handle something, and I revert to the lessons you taught me, about love, respect, determination and sheer will. She's so funny. Just like you. She is *so* funny. Do you know? Can you see her? Do you watch over her? If so, I'm gonna need you to go hang out with her in math class because somebody needs to explain it to her, so it makes sense. And while you're there, maybe put some of her suitors in check. Open a locker and smack them in the face or something. Just let them know you're there. It breaks my heart to know how much you wanted to be there. I remember you telling me that when you were diagnosed with cancer. That you just wanted to live long enough to watch her graduate high school. How I wish I could have made that happen. How I wish this disease hadn't moved so fast. How I wish everything was different. We're doing our best for her. You should know how many people love her, like really love her. She is surrounded by adults who care about her and are trying to keep her on the right path. So many.

But, in the still of the night, when life gets too hard, she still wants you. She wants her daddy. She still calls you that, you know. Her daddy. I guess that's what happens when you lose your dad young. She never transitioned into calling you "dad" or "pops" or "father" on a daily basis. You're always going to be "daddy" for that kid. Some days, I don't

17

know how to help her. Some days, I try to talk to her, and others, I try to leave her in her own moment. I think it's important to have time for both. Time to talk and reflect, and time to be quiet. I think you, of all people, would understand that.

I know how private you were, but I also know that your passion was helping people, and you told me that after you died, I could do whatever I wanted to with your story to help people. I'm trying, babe. *I am really trying.* At first, I thought I needed to bring awareness to pancreatic cancer, since that was the disease that stole you from us. And as I started doing that, and posting things on social media, the strangest thing happened. People started listening. Like, really listening. Suddenly, my newsfeeds were covered in purple and you would be shocked by all the people who started wearing purple in your honor in November, during pancreatic cancer awareness month. We started the #iam149 foundation, which gives back to pancreatic cancer patients. I am always excited to explain what "149" is, and when I tell people it's your badge number, I also get to add in how you were a police officer and how honorable you were. I get to tell them how you served our community faithfully, even when you were sick. It inspires people to know that you worked three weeks before your death, even full of tumors, and it makes people reevaluate their own struggles and tap into their own strengths. I don't think you ever knew what kind of impact you had on people during your battle, or what kind of impact you have now, but I will tell you, my love, you are a warrior. You are a respected, admired warrior and so many people have signed up to represent you now and carry on your story. I hope you are proud. Because there are thousands of "149's" now. You are not alone anymore in this fight. You are not alone.

But, something else happened, too. As I started sharing your story, I guess I was, subconsciously, also sharing mine. Ours. Our love story, and our grief. How it felt to lose you. How it feels to live without you. The lessons I have learned.

The chaos. The challenges. The successes. The gifts. The grief gifts. People started resonating with it. They started seeing their own story in mine and they started taking comfort that they were not the only person traveling this road. They started responding to the fact that some days are shit, and some days are amazing. They started to see that experiencing both of those days was ok. *It was ok to not be ok, and it was ok to be ok.*

I started getting messages from strangers asking me to keep telling this story. One of my favorites was from a woman who was grieving and who told me to *"please know that the bravery by which you are facing your life – it is helping some chubby drunk girl who wants to face plant onto a plate of Cheetos feel a little more encouragement about facing hers."* It struck me as funny, but more so – it was so real, *so damn real,* that I could not turn my back to it. So, I kept telling people. Anybody who would listen about you, about us, and about how you *can,* and you *will* survive even what seems like an insurmountable loss.

And guess what? During that time, it became more and more clear that grief was not reserved for somebody who lost somebody to death. No. Everybody is grieving. Everybody has suffered a loss, whether it's death, divorce, the loss of a job, a home, friends, or even just the idea of what we thought something was, they are grieving. It's all the same. It's the same cycle. The same emotions. The same process. No loss is worse than the other because *loss is loss.* Theirs hurts just as bad as mine. Everybody is living a "grief life" in some way. Everybody. And, if they can see tidbits of their story in mine, and gain insight in survival, then I know I am doing the right thing.

The more our story was out there, the more people it started helping, and so here I am. Writing this book to share it even further.

I hope that's ok with you. I hope you are proud of me. *I hope you are proud of us.*

21

Speaking of proud, we had a major winter storm last year, they were calling it the snow-apocalypse, or something. Somebody even made shirts for the survivors. No, I didn't get one, but I should have. Anyway, I learned how to clean off snow from the satellite dish. I had no idea it wasn't actually on top of the center of the house and was close enough to the side to just brush it off. I also learned you have to unhook the hoses from the house before they freeze. And, it's also beneficial to clean off all the ice on the windows on the car otherwise, when you open the window to order coffee, it falls inwards and on your lap.

Yes, baby, I'm learning. I am learning how to be a widow. I'm learning how to do it without you. I am learning how to survive. I am learning how to share that with other people and remind them that they are not alone in their grief, and that they will be ok. *They <u>will</u> be ok*, you know. I will be ok, too. But not one day goes by that I don't wish you were here.

Love, Me.

Chad

"A man is lucky if he is the first love of a woman. A woman is lucky if she is the last love of a man." Charles Dickens

He was my first love, and I was his last. Our hearts have always been connected, and the universe had a way of bringing us back together when we lost our way. I met Chad in the late spring of 1988, when we were both young teenage rebels living in the valley of Southern California. I had lived in a bubble most of my life, protected from the evils of the outside world. Some would say it was a charmed life, an idyllic childhood, but I was already experiencing grief, even as a young girl. My dad left when I was young, and while my mother did everything humanly possible to make that palatable, the loss of our family affected me in ways that I don't think any of us fully understood at the time. It was my first taste of grief and is something I carry with

24

me even today. It was one of the first things I thought of when Chad died, that we were robbing our children of the life we wanted them to have, and now could not give them because he was gone. It was so absolute. So final. So completely unfair. Like me, they were supposed to have two parents who loved each other and who raised them together and who offered them all the good things in the world.

I will never forget the day I met him. There are moments in time that are seared into our memories and this is one of them for me. Some days, I can't remember where I put my car keys, but I will never, ever forget the day I met Chad Register. Not ever.

It was a Tuesday, in April. I wasn't feeling well, and I specifically remember that I looked tired and didn't even try to hide it with make-up. I assume I was only at school that day because I had missed too many days to miss again, but I was spent. Completely exhausted. I asked a friend of mine, Yoshio, for a ride home. He obliged, and we walked out to the parking lot. I'm sure my mom will be horrified to know that his only method of transportation that day was a motorcycle, but I hopped on the back and waited for him to hand me a helmet. While he was putting his things away on his bike and prepping it to go, a little white sportscar pulled up. Yoshio got on the bike and I was so tired, I instinctively laid my head on his back, turning towards the car. Two high school boys were inside known to Yoshio, but not to me. They were from another school; one Yoshio had attended the year prior. Yoshio and the driver started talking, making plans for something and, when I finally got enough energy to open my eyes and look over at the passenger in the car, it happened.

Oh, how I wish I had done my make-up that day. He looked straight at me and smiled, kind-of nodding his head to say, "hello". He had a silly grin, one I would see a thousand more times in my life with him, and one I would adore just as much the last time as I did the first. I remember that my eye was a little bit swollen from whatever was making me sick that day, and hoped that when I smiled back, my squinty eye would look more alluring in the bright sun than freakish. It was before "duck lips" became popular but I'm pretty sure that I looked like an idiot trying to smile, squint and look as cool as he did. It was impossible to be as cool as he was. I would figure that out as the years went on. Nobody would ever be as cool as Chad was. Nobody.

He reminded me of the guy in Karate Kid movie, not the actual "Karate Kid" Ralph Macchio character, but the guy that beats him up in the first movie. I think his name was Johnny. And no, Chad wasn't a bully, nor did he beat people up on Halloween in the alleys of Reseda, but he kinda looked like him. Well, at least they had the same hair. Ok, go Google it, I'll wait.

I would come to find out that he drove a little red sports car, complete with a very, very loud sound system – one that would drive my neighbors crazy, but I didn't care. I just wanted to be with him, and nothing else mattered.

The afternoon in the parking lot came and went and, at some point, he asked Yoshio for my phone number, and asked Yoshio to give me his. I was not a shrinking violet. I was not afraid to make the first move. My mom told me to wait for him to call, but there was something about him that pulled me in so much, I couldn't wait. I didn't want to waste time. So, I called him one day. I was as polite as I could be when I asked for him and, subsequently, left a message because he was asleep. Turns out, he was always asleep, or always gone. I'm not even sure he ever called me back.

But he showed up. One day, he showed up. Back at the school, in his own car, leaning through the window asking me if I wanted a ride. Um, yes. Yes, I did. No girl was going to say no to that blonde, perfectly styled, coiffed hair, those piercing blue eyes, that "Hard Rock Café" sweatshirt, acid washed pegged jeans and that mysterious vibe. They just weren't. I wasn't. In fact, I learned over time that not many girls did say no, and even ones he wasn't asking would show up and sit on his doorstep waiting for him to come home. His friends would tell me he would sometimes have to park someplace else, and sneak in his house through the backyard to avoid the onslaught of teenage girls vying for his attention. At least I was allowed in the house.

He took me on dates. Ice cream dates. Movie dates. A big one to Sizzler when his dad gave him $20.00 and told him to take me "someplace nice". We spent the entire summer together, in the 80's, in the valley. It was something they made movies about. The days were hot, the nights were warm, and we drove, and drove, and drove around Los Angeles with the windows down and music blaring, singing until our voices were hoarse and our stomachs hurt from laughing. He could rap, you know. He might not have ever done it in front of anybody else, but he could rap. The last time we would drive like that and let the wind consume us while we sang at the top of

29

our lungs would be twenty-eight years later in Arizona, driving to a consultation for chemotherapy. In 2016, "Video Killed the Radio Star" immediately became my new favorite song. We were two decades older, but we were the same young kids who fell in love one summer a lifetime before.

When fall came, and school started, I was nervous. The night before my junior year, I was so anxious and, while talking to him on the phone, I said, "I just don't know if anybody will like me." He replied quickly with, "They will like you. I like you. In fact, I love you." That was the first of many, many times he would put my fears at ease, making everything alright, and fixing what was broken. He was that person for me. He made me feel safe. So secure. Without worry.

And, as the story goes with young love, we got wrapped up in rumors, drama and miscommunication and over the next few years broke up and got back together and broke up and got back together until, one day, we just said goodbye.

We had different lives then. We weren't playing "hokie pokie" in the rain anymore. We weren't playing poker in the park anymore. We weren't laughing and joking and having four-hour long phone calls in the middle of the night anymore. We weren't hanging out in Eaton Canyon with friends and being shooed out by the cops anymore. We weren't doing much of anything, except fighting, hurting each other and having too many toxic people around.

I remember the day that I met him, but I do not remember the last day I saw him as a teenager. Maybe I blocked it out. Maybe it was one of those moments that I could not bear to relive.

We went on with our lives, separately. I knew he moved to San Diego. I knew he had a baby with somebody else. I knew he was still close, but he was a lifetime away. I got married to somebody else, had two kids, and, eventually, divorced. It had been thirteen years since I knew Chad and I figured our time was gone. I figured our chance was done and over. Boy, was I wrong. And I have never been so happy to be wrong about something.

Because, on a sunny day in June 2002, a decade after we said "goodbye", after a simple email from him saying, "hello", we found each other again and committed to a life together.

With as much as a photog as I am, I don't have any pictures from my wedding day. There's a reason, which I will tell you, but it's weird not to have one piece of a photographic memory. Unrelated to that, I remember once I had a video tape of my 21st birthday and, accidentally, taped over it. I was crushed. But my mom told me that sometimes, the memories you have in your head and your heart are better anyway.

We didn't know it would be our wedding day. Chad and I woke up and went to breakfast. We were engaged and were planning a fall wedding. We had our eggs and toast and decided to head to the courthouse to see what we needed to do to get our marriage license. We drove to Van Nuys and asked our questions and he made a joke to a clerk that we should just find a judge to marry us that same day.

"Oh, no", she said. "We don't do weddings on Fridays."

We nodded and smiled and out of the corner of my eye, I saw an older couple standing in the corner. They had to be at least in their late 80's, her in a simple dress holding a very small, delicate bouquet, him standing beside her, in a dapper suit. Just standing there. Waiting.

Before we knew it, a Judge came out from behind the doors and made her way to them.

"Of course, I will marry you today". She told them.

The Judge extended her arm, as to show them the way, and the little couple shuffled behind her.

Our clerk, seeing this, shouted out to the Judge, while pointing at us. "These two want to get married as well". The Judge smiled and motioned for us to follow. I don't know who freaked out more, him or me.

Twenty minutes later, we were saying our vows to each other. We were both in shorts, t-shirts and flip flops as we said the words, "for better or worse, for richer or poorer, in sickness and in health, until death do us part".

We did just that. In the fourteen years we were married after that, we had all of those things. Every up and down. And we stuck with it. We made it until the end. We honored our vows to each other, and we will always be my favorite love story. We didn't get dressed up. I didn't have a bouquet. He didn't have a single rose pinned to his shirt. We didn't have a photographer. We didn't have camera phones then. We didn't have a lavish reception. We didn't even have cake. But in the end, it didn't matter. All that mattered was that we had each other.

Cancer stole my husband, but it did not steal our life. I think about that old couple every year. I fear I'm the only one of the four of us still left living. But, like every year, when I think of my own marriage I wish them a happy day as well.

Our first anniversary was spent in a hotel living it up, enjoying an exquisite dinner. Our last one was spent in a hospital room with a small pizza and cupcakes Chad couldn't eat. He died ten days after our last anniversary.

It was at the moment that I knew I would be happy to spend my anniversary with him anywhere, as long as we could spend it together.

And now, I spend them alone. And, while that is sad, and my heart hurts, I will reflect and remember the man he was, and the marriage we had. Because that marriage set the bar high for me. It wasn't always perfect, but it was perfection in my eyes.

I miss him. I miss him every day. I miss his laugh, his smile, his jokes, his charisma, his stories, his generosity, his support, his loyalty and above all, I just miss having him here.

I still walk around half awake searching for him. But I'm trying. I really am, like we all are.

The Grief Life

"Grief is in two parts. The first is loss. The second is the remaking of life." – Anne Roiphe

When I first read the phrase, "Grief Life", I actually stopped what I was doing and sat back in my chair and absorbed it. I closed my eyes, took it in, read it again and out of the blue, everything clicked. Everything suddenly made sense.

I realized in that instant, that we're all living a grief life in some way. It's inevitable, honestly. We are all walking this life carrying some kind of grief, dealing with some kind of loss or uncertainty. The professionals have sometimes thrown grief in the same general category as depression, but I'm not sure I totally believe that's all that it is. I think grief and depression go hand in hand, but at the same time, I don't think grief is something we can cure with behavioral therapy or medication. Can it help? Sure. But is there a cure? No, I don't think so. I think we have to learn to live our life walking along side it, as opposed to constantly trying to walk around it, or even through it. I just don't think it goes away. But, I do think you can live a fulfilling, beautiful, hysterical life with it.

A friend of mine reminded me recently that, unless somebody dies very young, they will experience grief at some point in their life. The loss of a parent, grandparent, spouse, child, friend; we're all bound to feel grief as a result of losing somebody to death. I agree with this and challenge to take that idea further. For me, I do not think that grief from loss is exclusive to death.

Loss is loss.

Whether that's the loss of a loved one, a divorce, the loss of a job, or even just the idea of what you think something was going to be, losing it changes everything. It produces the same feelings – the same confusion and hurt and healing from any loss takes you down the same road. There is no roadmap that directs people grieving a death to go to

37

the right, and people grieving a divorce to go to the left. We're all traveling down a difficult path and hoping to someday find a place of peace.

I had a therapist not long ago tell me that the grieving process—reference the loss of a loved one—does not start until that person dies.

I must have been a sight to her. For a good five minutes, I sat there with my mouth open and my eyes blinking trying to focus on what she had just said. I was rendered speechless, which is something that rarely happens to me.

I finally found my voice again and mustered a meek, "Excuse me?"

She leaned forward, folded her hands together in her lap. and repeated it.

"I don't care what anybody says, the grief process does not start at the time of diagnosis."

Really? Are you serious? Really? In my mind, I knew she was wrong, but it also prompted me to question if she meant that if somebody doesn't actually die, you don't get to grieve?

Late January 2015, my husband had jaundice. We knew something was wrong, but not once did I allow my brain to go to the idea of pancreatic cancer until the ER doctor told us there was a mass on his pancreas.

The world stopped. At least mine did. His did. People rushed by doing their jobs, talking about what they were doing that weekend, yet my eyes were fixed on the doctor in front of me who was explaining what was happening. Her lips were moving but everything was in slow motion. Sounds were coming out of her mouth. I assume they were words, but I can't remember any of them.

I do, however, remember her face. It's burned into my memory forever. I remember how she took a deep breath before she said it. I remember how she cocked her head to the side. I remember how she slightly shrugged her shoulders. I remember she made this weird sound before she delivered the news.

I remember Chad's reaction, and I remember feeling like I had just been hit by a truck.

Do you think I took the same person home from the hospital two days later that I brought in, therapist lady? Do you think my husband walked into the house and sat on the bed and flipped on the TV and had a beer? Do you think my kids' dad was there when they all came around to see what happened? Do you think I was the same? My children?

No. No. And no, again. We lost him that day. We lost the man who held our future, our stories, our jokes, and our memories. Over the next 18 months we would see parts of him again, but we would never fully have him back.

The diagnosis changed everything. It changed him. It changed me. It changed the kids. It changed our plans. It changed the atmosphere. It redefined everything.

And the grief process started.

It's not just about the loss of someone the day they die. It's about the loss of the life you've built together, the loss of security. The loss of uncontaminated fun. The loss of knowing what was supposed to be, because suddenly, everything you knew is no longer within your grasp. I had people before this tell me they were envious of my marriage. Of the life we had. And out of nowhere, my life came crashing down around me.

I've been called selfish for feeling this way. After all, I wasn't the one diagnosed. What right did I have to feel like I was losing in this equation?

You're right. I was not the one diagnosed. But, I can't tell you how much it feels like we all were. We all died in some way.

We tried everything. We fought that monster. We cried. We reached out to every scientist we could get an email for. We tried to be normal in the middle of it. We both worked. Kids did their school, sports, whatever it was; we went on.

But we were never the same.

And when he died, my grief became more pronounced, but it didn't start there, nor did it end there. It was just "different". Maybe it was more real. Maybe it was more tangible. But it wasn't new.

I've said it many times--I don't think there is a hierarchy to grief. I think there are some things that are more unnatural, like the loss of a child, or the death of a young spouse, but I don't think anybody's grief outweighs somebody else's.

We lose something important to us, and we cycle through the same process. As I said before, during any kind of loss we experience the same feelings. Could it be that death brings us a harsher realty? Yes, for sure. But I stand by my opinion that the process is the same.

I don't know how you're supposed to cope. I think we all do that differently in our own time. I think we do what's right for us at that moment. I think we all figure it out one way or another.

But what I think we don't do enough of is realize that people are hurting when you don't even know it. People are feeling deep feelings of grief, even if their person is still alive or even if they're

42

dealing with a different kind of loss. People are still struggling to get out of bed some days because those feelings, no matter what is causing them are hard. Really hard.

I was very lucky to have a ton of support at the end of Chad's illness and after he died. And as I move on, I still have more support than I ever thought I would. I don't know why. Maybe because I am very vocal about how I feel, or maybe because I am open to the help, but it is not lost on me that I am so fortunate, even in the midst of what feels like, at times, a nightmare.

But, it's not a nightmare all the time. It still hurts somedays more than I want to admit. The experience has triggered a lot of anxiety. I'm more guarded. I'm tired. I feel really unmotivated sometimes. But when I look deeper into this, and realize that I am not alone, there are some days where I actually feel really good. And that's when I appreciate being aware of my grief life, and in a

43

strange way, I am beginning to appreciate all it has to offer.

I don't think there is one person out there who isn't walking this life with some kind of grief. We all have "what-if's" and "should haves" and some of us have suffered through big things.

I hope as you read about my grief life that you can insert your own story into mine. I hope that if you recognize some of the stories, some of the feelings and some of the emotions that you will not just see that there is a way to cope, but that you will also see the value in this whole crazy journey we are all on – and that we really are in this together.

The nightmare begins

"Worst nightmares can also appear with your eyes open." – Florence Welch

When Chad was first diagnosed with pancreatic cancer, I was sure he was going to beat it. I know that having that diagnosis sounds like an automatic death sentence, but after doing some research, while the prognosis was grim, I found out there were people surviving it. There were long term survivors. And even if the five-year survival rate was 1%, I was certain he would be in that 1%. I convinced myself of that for a very long time. So, when he actually died, it was a shock. It was expected, but it wasn't.

In January 2015, we were in Las Vegas for our daughter's gymnastics meet. At the time, she was a competitive gymnast and we traveled all over. Between that, work and real life, it wasn't uncommon for us to be tired a lot. But, on this trip, he was more tired than normal and complained quite a bit about not feeling well. He thought it was something he ate and just wanted to sleep it off. We got back from our trip and life went back to normal, but about a week later, he started turning yellow. So much so that one of his co-workers commented something to him about it. Now, my husband never went to the doctor. And when I say "never", I mean it. He went one time when he was forced to do a physical to be hired as police officer, but other than that, he really never went. After he brought up the yellowing to me, I noticed it too and quickly saw that it was in his eyes. The only thing I know about when it comes to yellowing of the skin is jaundice. So, I Googled it. Most of the results were liver issues and hepatitis, which would make sense considering that, in his line of work, it's easy to contract diseases when arresting people. I made him a doctor's appointment, but he went by himself because neither of us thought it was really anything to worry about. He would get some medicine, or it would resolve on its own.

Never did we think it could be cancer. After his appointment, he told me the doctor agreed it could be hepatitis and did a hepatitis panel and would have the results in a few days. After a couple of days, it got worse. He was getting more yellow. I called the doctor and explained it to them and they told me they were just about to call because the blood work came back negative. My heart sunk a little bit, but I still didn't think about cancer because he was a 44-year-old strong, healthy police officer. Cancer wasn't even on my radar.

However, looking back, I do remember the urgency in his voice. "We need to get him to the hospital for a CT scan." I told Chad and he refused, which was no surprise. He did not want to go to the hospital and he most certainly did not want to go to the hospital in the community in which we lived and take a chance of running into anybody he knew. Look, I'm a pretty persuasive person but it took everything I had to convince him to go to another hospital further away. When we got there, we sat in

47

the parking lot for a good half hour, me trying to convince him to go in, him not wanting to.

I didn't start getting scared until we walked in through the lobby doors and up to the nurse's desk to check in. I told them the doctor sent him for some tests, and they responded with, "Is this James?" (James was his given name). That's about the time I almost passed out on the floor. I knew it was serious if the doctor called ahead. I said it was, they immediately took him back, got him prepped and took him for an ultrasound. I went into the room with him and as they did the test, we both earnestly tried to follow along with what the technician was doing, or how long she stayed focused on one place. When she started measuring things, I immediately flashed back to when I was pregnant and how, during ultrasounds, they would measure the size of the baby. *"What in the hell is she measuring?"*

We would find out later that it was a tumor. After we went back into the ER room, the doctor came in and told him that she couldn't see anything well enough and wanted to take him back for a CT. The doctor told me it would be quick and to wait in the room for him. Again, I didn't think much about it. They hadn't said anything. Nobody even hinted anything. They rolled him out and as I sat there in that cold room, the ER doctor walked in.

I will never forget the look on her face. I will never forget how her lips were pursed together or how she cocked her head to the side and subtly shrugged her shoulders. I will never forget how deep of a breath she drew in or the weird sound she pushed out of her mouth before she spoke.

"We've found what we think is about a 3-centimeter tumor on his pancreas."

She could have been the nicest person in the world, but at that moment, I hated her. She became my enemy. She represented nothing for me except panic, fear, and shock. I wanted to punch her in the face. I hated her face. I can still see it in my mind. If I saw her on the street, I would know her. I would recognize her in any crowd and I would still hate her.

It wasn't her fault this happened, but her face was the representation of everything bad and to this day, I can't shake it. They say that certain things are burned into your memory during a crisis, and her face is one of those things. She was the first tangible thing I saw during our crisis. I've often thought about seeking her out. I have thought about just going to the ER to see her, but I am afraid what emotion it might illicit. Because throughout his 18-month ordeal, there are some things I remember and some I don't, but I will never forget her face, or what the room looked like where I was sitting, or how she didn't seem to know what to do.

"I am not going to tell him until we get the results back from the CT, in about 45 minutes."

The hell you aren't.

There was no way, NO WAY, I was sitting in that room with my husband for 45 minutes and not telling him what they think was going on. And there was no way I was telling him by myself. As I recall this event, I remember she shrugged her shoulders then, too. She said I could tell him if I wanted to, but she wasn't going to until she knew for sure. Do they teach shoulder shrugging in medical school? Maybe try sitting down and looking me in the eye? I don't remember exactly how the conversation went, but I do remember telling her that she was going to tell him. We weren't keeping it from him and I was not informed enough to answer his questions. She reluctantly agreed and when he returned, she told him.

He nodded, and said, "okay."

Pure grit, that man. Pure grit.

I saw him processing it in his head, and I saw him trying to make sense of it. It was quiet for a moment and I don't think anybody knew what to say. We sat in that silence, as questions raced in my head. *So, now what? Where do we go? He can have surgery, right? We will just fix this, right? It will all be ok, right?* I don't know what he was thinking but I am guessing it was along those same lines.

51

Out of nowhere, the doctor decided to break the silence. "Do you have kids?" she asked him.

I shot a look at her. Really? That's what you're going to ask him right now? If he has kids?

He cleared his throat to answer her. "Yes, four." It only took seconds for the tears to come. From him. It was the only time I would see him cry during his eighteen-month ordeal, and it is something I will never, ever forget. And I will never forget the feeling I had of wanting to tackle that doctor right then and there. I think when somebody hurts the person you love, you can't help but want to attack. Like I said, I know this wasn't her fault. I know there was no good way to tell him. But in an instant, she just became the association to me between life and death. The rest of our time in that 8x8 room is a blur. I don't recall anything. The next thing I remember is being in the actual hospital room they were keeping him overnight in. I did not want to go home. I did not want to shower or eat or do anything but sit there with him. It was a Friday, and my older kids were off doing whatever older kids do and my younger daughter was at a sleepover with a teammate as they had a competition the next day. I was not going anywhere. But, for some reason, I felt like he needed pajamas. I don't know why. He could have stayed in a hospital gown, but I was bound and determined to get him pajama bottoms. And a real toothbrush. Deodorant. I didn't know how long he would be there and I would be damned not to have some creature comforts for him. At some point, when his mom was there with him, I went to the store. I walked to the car, still not totally processing what had happened. I got in the car and called my boss. I had to tell her I wasn't coming to work, but she had also lost her husband a few years before that and, for some reason, I vomited the whole story on her. She talked to me. Consoled me. Let me cry. Told me how to get to the store because I was in a place I wasn't familiar with and had no idea where I was going. And, after my crying session on the phone, she told me to wash my face, get the pajamas and

53

then go back and figure out how we were going to fight this thing. She had faith in me. I'm glad one of us did.

I called the mother of the friend who my daughter was staying with. I don't remember if I gave specifics, but I asked her to keep my daughter for the weekend. She agreed.

It was the first of many, many, many fires I would be putting out over the next year and a half and the first of many arrangements I would have to make revolving around this cancer. From that point forward, my life was figuring things out, making appointments, reading articles, sending emails to doctors, praying for trials, and trying to find a cure. I became obsessed with saving him. One minute I was a wife and busy working mother and the next, I was a crazed maniac just trying to figure out what to do. But, more importantly, I became his advocate; a role I will never regret.

When I got back to the hospital, he told me that the doctors were going to perform something called an ERCP to look at the tumor and put stents in his bile duct.   Apparently, the reason he was jaundiced was because the tumor was blocking the duct. He also told me that he fully expected me to go to our daughter's gymnastics meet the following day.

"You're crazy," was the only thing I could think to say.

He insisted, and, in the end, he won. There were three gymnastics moms I told about what was going on and begged them not to say anything to anybody. They met me outside and prayed with me and then walked me in, like, literally, took my hand and walked me into the meet. If you have ever been to a gymnastics meet, you know how stressful it can be. It's scary to watch your kid out there flipping around and doing tricks on a balance beam that is four inches in width. But that night, my panic and fear weren't about gymnastics. It was about my husband lying in a hospital bed wondering if he was going to live or die. I remember sitting in my seat, one of my friends holding my hand while another mom who I didn't know as well sat on the other side of me. There was no way I could hide my stress and, eventually, the tears came. The other mom leaned over to me and asked if I was ok. I told her I was, but I still couldn't stop crying. At some point, she leaned in again and whispered something to me about "men" and "breakups" and I guess she assumed Chad and I were having problems, but man, what I would have done to be having those kinds of problems over potential dying problems.

I went back to the hospital after the meet, surprised to find him sitting straight up and on his iPad. Before I could even sit down, he turned his iPad towards me and pointed at a picture of a doctor, along with a biography. It was for Dr. John Cameron, a pancreatic cancer specialist at Johns Hopkins in Maryland. He said to me, with no reservation, "I don't care if he says I can or can't have surgery, I want to hear it from him."

I don't know how long I stood there with my jaw on the ground, but it seemed like an eternity before I could speak. I would do anything for this man. Anything. But how in the world was I going to get him across the country to Johns Hopkins of all places *and* get him an appointment with one of the premiere cancer surgeons in the world? It's not that he wasn't physically strong enough to get there, but how do you even make this happen?

Well, you pick up the phone. My first round of phone calls to Johns Hopkins was an automated messaging service telling me to leave my information and somebody would get back to me. I think I left four or five of those. Then, somebody said they would get back to me in seventy-two hours.

No.

Five minutes felt like five days. Seventy-two hours would have been excruciating. There was no way we could wait that long for an answer. Both of us felt like our insides were crawling out of our skin – the anxiety and fear was winning. We were not waiting. I took to Google, and my intention was to find an email for the doctor. There wasn't one. So,

I looked up all the email addresses at Johns Hopkins and, using the address after the @ symbol, I tried to figure out what his email was using his first name then last name and last name then first name and so on. Nothing worked. I wasn't giving up. I just wasn't. I composed an email explaining our situation and sent it out to every email I could find for Hopkins. I didn't care if the custodian got it. I believed in the goodness of people and somebody would see it and forward it to the right place.

And guess what? They did. About ten minutes later, I got a phone call from a lady named Mary. I don't know what she did there, but she gave me the list of things I needed to do. Get his medical records. Get a CD of the imaging tests. Do this, do that. I furiously wrote down a list. And while I was prepared to do it, it was overwhelming. I don't know if it was because she could hear my voice breaking or the constant "mom, mom, mom" coming from the background in my house but, suddenly, she just said,

"You know what? I will take care of it. Give me the hospital's name and I will take care of it."

Two days later, I received the call from Dr. Cameron's office. They wanted Chad to come out the next week to meet with him. I am sure there was an easier way to make an appointment, but I have never been so happy for an invitation to Maryland in my whole life. They had reviewed his medical records, looked over the imaging, and they thought they could help him.

I remember meeting Dr. Cameron for the first time. He graduated Harvard in 1958. I am not very good at math, but I quickly did the numbers in my head and by my calculations, in 2015 when we were there, that would have meant he graduated some 57 years prior. Then, I tried to figure out how old he might have been at the time. I don't know, 22? So, was he born in 1937? Was he 78? And he was going to perform surgery? I mean, I trusted him. I read up on him. But, he's 78, right? The door opened, and he shuffled in. Nothing in his hands. No files, just a

PA who was following him. He sat down. I looked straight down at his hands to make sure he wasn't shaking or anything. Nothing. Solid as a rock. He looked at Chad and said, "You're from Idaho?" Chad nodded. "I had a PA that moved to Idaho. Maybe you know her." Chad smiled. "Is that an 'Under Armour' shirt you're wearing?" Chad nodded again. "You know the factory is here in Baltimore. There's an outlet store. You should check it out." He settled into his chair before addressing him again. Still, no notes. No file.

"You're 44?"

"Yes."

"Married." That wasn't a question. It was a statement along with, "And you have four kids." Again, no notes.

"Yes."

"And, you're a police officer?"

"Yes."

"That explains the 'Under Armour' shirt." They both smiled. I think Chad even chuckled.

"You have about a 3- centimeter tumor at the head of your pancreas. I am not totally sure yet where it's coming from. It is either coming from the pancreas or the duodenum. I have looked over your records. We don't see any other tumors. Can you do surgery in two weeks?"

YES.

Over the next thirty minutes, Dr. Cameron described to us in detail what the Whipple Surgery was. How they were going to take apart his intestines, remove the tumor, and put his digestive system back together in a bypass.

Two weeks later, we sat anxiously waiting in the surgery prep room talking, trying to joke around with each other, laughing and completely avoiding the fact that he was about to embark on an eight-hour procedure that would likely determine whether he would live or die. We spoke nothing at that moment of anything realistic, as he had given me clear instructions the night before on certain practical things. There was no need to rehash it all. There was nothing we could do. In fact, the reality of that morning did not set in until the nurses came in and told him to remove his jewelry.

He slipped his wedding band off and handed it to me.

I pulled in a deep breath.

I swallowed hard.

My heart shook.

I bit my lip and smiled.

He smiled back.

The next time I would hold his wedding ring was the week before he died, eighteen months later. Looking back, I now realize how sick he was but, at the time, I still didn't want to see it. He had experienced a stroke and after they let him come home, I had to take him back to the hospital every few days to the heparin clinic to get shots to prevent any more blood clots. He was so weak I ended up having to push him in a wheelchair and after one appointment, after we left, he mentioned he thought he lost his wedding ring inside the office. We went back in, couldn't find it and I asked him again where he thinks he lost it.

"I don't know. I just heard it hit the ground."

He was confused. He was tired. I couldn't even be upset. I touched his hand and leaned in close to him. "We will find it. It's ok". My heart said we would. My brain knew we wouldn't. Right then and there I accepted the fact that he was going to die, and he was going to do that without his ring.

He insisted we retrace our steps at the hospital, and we did. I pushed him through the hospital, the entire length of it, while he scanned the floor and corners for any sparkle that might catch his eye. We told security. We left our name at lost and found. We went home.

We did not speak about it again. He felt bad about it, and my heart was broken. There was no point in talking about either one of those things. I tried to reassure him that it was ok, but I don't think he believed me. It wouldn't be the first time in this awful journey that I tried to make something ok, even when it wasn't. I didn't want him to worry. I didn't want him to ever think I had given up hope.

I found places to break down without him seeing me. The shower, parking lots, in the car—anyplace where he wouldn't notice. A few days before he died, it was the laundry room. Sleep deprived and scared, I carried the laundry in there, put it in the machine and paused before opening the door to leave.

This was going to be the last time I would ever wash his shirts.

My mind could not handle that information. I could not process it fast enough. I could not process it slow enough. I wanted to throw up. I had been washing his shirts for fifteen years and, on that day, I stood in the laundry room and was hit with the reality that I would never wash his things again. Throughout our marriage, there were times I was annoyed I had to wash his shirts. There were times I was irritated that his shirts were left in the dryer. There were times I didn't want to wash them. And

64

in this moment, *this very moment,* I promised God that if he let Chad live, that I would never be irritated with washing his shirts again.

But it was true. I will never wash his shirts again.

I don't know how long it took me to slide to the ground, but with my back against the wall and my knees drawn to my chest, I bawled. I sobbed until I could not breathe. I instinctively covered my mouth to disguise any of the prehistoric sounds coming from my gut because, even though he was heavily medicated and asleep, I still could not take the chance of him finding out I was slowly giving up hope.

There is this weird calming feeling your body has after you have cried like that. Your face gets swollen. Your lips tingle. Your eyes can't blink. Your voice is quiet. Your thoughts slow down. You take deep breaths. You cleanse yourself. And, in that moment of deep despair, you look around and memorize your surroundings and the things close to you. Up to the ceiling, down the walls, at the washing machine filling with water, then down to the floor. And suddenly, you see it.

A perfect, platinum wedding ring.

And the crying starts again as you pick it up and squeeze it into your hand, holding it close to your chest, grasping it as tight as you can, vowing you will never lose it again.

The Grief Gift

"Someone I loved once gave me a box full of darkness. It took me years to understand that this too, was a gift." Mary Oliver

Dear Chad,

You know what phrase is really hard to digest? "Everything happens for a reason". I guess I believe this to some degree. I think it's true in a lot of ways. Either that, or we use it to justify why something is happening in our lives, whether it be right or wrong. I think I lean towards believing in it; timing, fate and being able to look back on an event and have it all make sense later. Whatever happened ten years ago catapulted you into a cycle where when you look back on it now, you can see why all these things had to happen to get where you are today. But, even with all that, the one thing I do not understand, and maybe I never will, is why this happened to you, and why you died.

Very early on after you were diagnosed, we both decided not to ask why. We knew the answer was futile. In fact, we knew there was no good answer. We knew that we would never really know and that even if we did figure it out, it would just never make sense. It was unfair. It was unfair to you. To me. To the kids. To your family. To your friends. To pretty much everybody. I'm not afraid to say that. I know life isn't fair, and maybe I sound like a four-year old stomping their feet after getting a smaller serving of dessert, but I don't care. It wasn't fair, and I am never going to look back and think it was.

Since you died, so many others I have known have followed suit. When you were alive, I belonged to a bunch of cancer support groups and, one by one, the people who I connected with online and became friends with, just started dying. And, so many people I know in my personal life started experiencing grief and sharing that with me. It's like there's no getting away from it.

Since then, I've been trying to figure out what grief is. How do you deal with it? When does it begin? When does it end? What is the process? Is it the same for everyone? Does anybody even know what to do? Does a counselor have the answers? Does a priest? What about another widow or widower? A fatherless child? A childless parent? Does anybody really have a clear definition of it?

What I've found is, the answer is no. Nobody really knows your grief. They know their own. They know what loss feels like, but the only person that can feel your tragedy is you. And your tragedy is never secondary to somebody else's. Somebody else's loss may be different than my loss, but it is truly the biggest thing in your life which far outshines the loss somebody else is experiencing, as it should be. I don't care if it's the loss of a parent or a spouse, a child, a friend, a dog -- people should allow themselves to grieve on the same level as somebody who's loss "seems" more significant. *What's significant to a person is important.*

But how do you deal with it? What's right and what's wrong? I think some of us feel like we're stagnant. It's like moving in slow motion while the rest of the world flies by. You want to grab ahold of everybody and shake them and scream for them to stop. We're not ready for life to just go on as normal. For others, it's being proactive. Finding things to stay busy, getting involved in a cause, or finding ways to honor the one you love. For some, it's easier to wipe your hands clean and just move on. Maybe thinking about it is too painful, that it does more harm than good. And still others will never move on and others will never give into their grief.

For me, I'm all of those things wrapped into one. *I think about it. I don't think about it. I get involved. I shut down. I cry. I laugh. I hold on. I let go.*

Maybe there isn't just one clear definition of how to grieve or how to deal. Maybe it's a personal process we all have to figure out on our own. Maybe, it's about the amazing lessons we get to learn. Maybe they are gifts from grief. *A grief gift.*

1. **I no longer care what people think**. I love and respect the opinions of others, especially those close to me, but in the end, I don't care anymore if they think I'm right or wrong in any decision or choice I make. It's been incredibly freeing.

2. **Along with that, I've removed people from my life who don't fit anymore**. I no longer have the time or patience to deal with people that don't want to be part of my life, or who cause undue stress or angst for me or my children.

3. **I allow myself time to grieve, and then I give myself permission to pick myself up and move on.** It's ok to move past it. It's ok to put it away sometimes. And, it's ok to take it out sometimes.

4. **I won't now, or ever, seal off my heart.** I loved you with a kind of passion not easily explained. You were my person. You knew me better than anyone and you understood me. People liked being around us because we were funny. We had fun. But, I will not harden my heart because of it. I know it would be devastating to you for me to stop living. And it would be unnatural to stop loving. I'm fortunate that I experienced the kind of love we had that makes me someday want to experience it again.

5. **We will never be victims of this.** My children and I will forge ahead because that's what we do. We will reflect, and remember, and hurt and heal but we will never be victims. We will never ask "why", but rather we will turn our crisis into something inspirational.

6. **I will figure out how to be independent of you.** I no longer see everything I have to learn as stumbling blocks or hurdles. I see them as great

adventures chalked full of interesting experiences. Perception is key.

7. **I will find my way.** At times I feel like I'm fumbling around in the dark, and other times I feel as if I'm walking straight ahead with purpose. Both of these are ok. Both of them work. My failures will lead me to the right answers eventually.

8. **I will mourn you.** I will think of you every day and silently wish you were here, and I will surround myself only with people who understand and support that.

9. **I will find balance.** I will figure out how to love and miss you while nurturing myself and others.

10. **I will accept it.** I will hate that acceptance, but I will do it, and it will empower me

and the kids. I will give up on the "what-ifs", and "we should haves", and will accept what is.

So many people are affected by grief, and I recognize that. So many people are affected daily by their own hard times, and I recognize that as well. And, I will challenge people not to give up hope. Ever. They cannot give up on themselves. And as they face this awful reality, I want them to know they will survive. It will be hard. They will fall down. And, then, they will get back up. But, they will survive. Day after day, I am presented with a new challenge, a new problem, a new hurdle and I do not have you here to help me, which makes no sense. You were supposed to be here. You were supposed to take care of me. But, somehow, Babe, I am learning how to take care of myself, and I will survive too. I promise.

Love,
Me

For the Caretakers

"Being deeply loved by someone gives you strength,
while loving someone deeply gives you courage."
Lao Tzu

After my husband died of pancreatic cancer, I created a foundation in his name. I did this because I refused to let his death be in vain, and I wanted to try to find a way to directly help other pancreatic cancer patients. I do not regret it for one second, but by doing so, it keeps me in the center of all things cancer, which includes following the stories, and sometimes having to process the deaths of people near and far who I have come to love. That part sucks. I can tell you that. I am frustrated and angry with cancer, but I am so tired of losing my friends.

Recently, we received another devastating blow. Another friend dead because of pancreatic cancer. I grieve with his family, and it has brought up so many difficult memories. Memories and facts that

75

maybe I wasn't totally prepared to talk about before, but I am now.

This chapter is for the caretakers who are left behind. Those amazing, beautiful, selfless souls that dedicated their lives to the welfare of another human being. The superheroes behind the scenes. The men and women who sacrificed everything in their own life to try to save the life of the person they love. It's not just about caretakers taking care of terminally ill patients. It's about anybody that is taking care of anybody who is struggling. I want you to know how much admiration and respect I have for you, but I also want you to know this:

Nobody will really "get it" unless they have done it. People might say they do, but nobody will truly understand what you did, day in and day out unless they have done it themselves. You're not a nurse, even though you might have been acting as one, but caretaking goes so far above just caring for somebody physically. I know how much you have worried, how many questions you have asked, how many doctors you have talked to, how many sleepless nights you have had, how many times you have questioned your decisions, how many food recipes you have tried, how many supplements you bought, how many personal events you missed, how many times you have told your friends, "I can't tonight", how many trips you didn't plan, how many excuses you've made, how many specialists you sought out, how many emails you've sent, how many times you have slept on a chair in a hospital room, how many times you have stayed up all night watching them breathe, how many times you felt foggy and exhausted because you forgot to eat that day, how many times you memorized their face in case it was the last time you would see it, how many times you cried yourself to sleep, how many times you have said you were "fine", how many times you felt like you could not do one-more-thing, how many times your stomach has cramped because you're not drinking enough water, how many times you wished you had an answer either way—good or bad—and felt guilty about that, how many times you didn't wash your hair because you didn't have enough time or energy, how many times you have thought about what life might be like if you weren't doing this, how many times you have prepared yourself for the worst, how many times you caught yourself dreaming about the best outcome, how many times you cursed the universe and how many times you just wanted to sleep and felt guilty about that, too. I get it. I've felt every single one of these. I have felt good, I've felt bad, happy, depressed, relieved, motivated, tired. I have felt like we were going to win, and I have felt like we were going to lose. But, the person who has never done what you do, sacrificed what you have sacrificed, lived the life you have lived will never understand. It's not that they don't want to try to "get it". It's not that they won't support you the best they can. But they will never be able to internalize what it feels like. Consider talking to other caretakers about how you feel – somebody who really gets it, while reserving other stuff for other people. People want to help. They want to feel needed. They want to do what they can do. They just, sometimes, have to be assigned the right tasks. But as people are really trying, give them grace when they fumble and make mistakes.

Speaking of Grace: As caretakers, we are often telling each other "give yourself a break." Whether our person is alive or passed on, this is one piece of advice that is constantly handed out. I nod every time I hear it but, inside, I just laugh and laugh and laugh and then laugh some more. Heck, I have even said the line to people, but I think I mean it differently than the way it's meant. When I say it, I don't mean "sit on the couch, put your feet up, break out your bon-bons and tune out the world" (even though you should). What I really mean is, give yourself some grace. I know who we are. I know our personality types. I know we're not going to, literally, "take a break." It's not really who we are. We are on the go all the time, and if we're not organizing something, we're worrying about organizing something. It's too hard to sit down. It's too hard to shut our minds off. It's too hard not to figure out the next step. We're going to be tired. We're going to be cranky. We're going to change the way we think about certain things. We're going to care less about certain things anymore and care more about others. We're going to forget things. We're going to buy cupcakes for our kids' class instead of making them. We might even forget to buy them. We're going to cry at commercials because we're overwhelmed. We're going to be snippy sometimes. We're even going to sometimes wish it wasn't us. Yep, I said it. We are sometimes going to wish *it was not us.* And, boy, we're gonna beat ourselves up for that one. In that moment, in that awful, guilty moment, you must learn how to give yourself grace. You have to. You have to let yourself feel what you feel, and then forgive yourself. You have to give yourself a break. That kind of break. It is ok, and completely normal to feel that. It is ok to feel it all. You are dedicated and committed to a scary, uncertain, and possibly sad journey. Give yourself some grace. Feel the feeling and move on. Process it and then put your head back in the game. Don't get stuck there. You can, and you will do it and you will be ok.

If it's over: I am not saying that your loved one won't be successful in their battle. Please don't read into this. But, for those of you who have lost them, this is for you. I am mad at myself that I felt a tinge of relief when it was done. I don't even like talking about it. It makes me feel gross. I actually hate that I felt that way. My husband, the man whom I loved almost my whole life, died and there was a flash of a moment where it was a relief. I can tell you I felt that way because he wasn't in pain anymore, or whatever smoke I want to blow up your ass, but the truth is, I was relieved that we finally had the answer. For so long we were living in limbo that the limbo was killing us faster than the cancer. I remember him telling me once, "I don't care if it's good or bad, I just want the answer." It was the not knowing that was so hard. It was the constant wondering that was so hard. So that last week when we were in the hospital, and he was struggling so much, and nobody knew what to do or what was going to happen, I just wanted it over. I wanted it over for him, and I wanted it over for me. Call me selfish, tell me how awful I am – I don't care. You can't say anything to me that I haven't already said to myself. You can't beat me up more than I already have. The last few days, I begged the doctors to do something. I wiped his brow. My daughter helped him drink ice tea. We went through the motions, but I knew he was dying. I asked them to start chemo anyway. I prayed. I cried. I froze sometimes, but I wanted them to try everything. I had hope. I reluctantly signed a DNR only because they told me CPR would kill him anyway. I still hate myself for that. I still wish they had brought him back and kept him alive until they came up with a treatment or even a cure. I can't stand how I felt in that moment. I even talked to his other doctors, other oncologists, and other surgeons after he died to ask them what they would have recommended. They all said that they would have let him go and signing the DNR was the right thing to do, but even then – I still hate myself for it. Yet, at the same time, when it was over, there was this awful, sick sense of relief. It was over. We didn't have to worry anymore. We didn't have to waste hope. We didn't have to figure one more thing out. It was just over. I just wanted to sleep. And I felt like the worst person in the world. The feeling didn't last long but it bothered me that it was there at all anyway. But, since then, after talking to other caretakers, I have found that it's normal. Can you believe that? Normal? All of these feelings, the confusion, the internal conflict – *it's normal.* Apparently, you CAN feel a variety of emotions, even ones that don't make sense. And then, guess what? Even though you're not taking care of them anymore, you're still functioning in the same manner as you were before. Suddenly, you have a funeral to plan and finances to figure out and paperwork to do and you dive right into it because it's *what you do, it's what you have trained yourself to do, it's what you have been doing,* and those people who have never done what you have wonder how you can be so callous and matter-of-fact, when the truth is – it's all you know anymore. All you know how to do is to take control and do whatever you have to do. You've learned how to set your emotions aside and handle the crisis and figure it out step-by-step. You have learned how to function in chaos. You have learned how to take care of everything and everybody in spite of your fear, your sadness and your loss. And, consequently, people will judge you. You will be too cold. Too heartless. Too robotic. They will say things about you and whisper when you walk by because they don't know. They have no idea. Pay no mind to those people. They have no idea, and I know you don't want them to know what it feels like because then they will know what kind of life this is. Then they will know what this kind of loss feels like. I don't wish that on anybody. Not even the people who don't understand me. Nobody should have to live that kind of reality.

My dear friends who are still doing the selfless act of caretaking: Be proud of yourself. Know that what you are feeling is OK. Know that you are doing something that not everybody can do. But above all, be kind to yourself. Know you're normal. And please, please give yourself a break.

Forgetting what he sounded like

"Beauty exists not in what is seen and remembered, but in what is felt and never forgotten." Johnathan Jena

It's sad to admit that, but it's true. I am slowly forgetting what he sounded like. What he felt like. How he laughed.

Chad was a magical storyteller. He was so funny, it was like being involved in a stand-up comedy routine on a daily basis. He wasn't obnoxious in any way. He wasn't loud. In fact, most people would have probably said he was "shy" because he was very quiet until he got to know you. But, he was subtly funny, all the time. Whether it was a look he would give you, or a laugh he would share, or a phrase he would use or words he made up, he was so funny. He had a cadence that was second to none, in my opinion. He didn't need a stage. He didn't really even need any material. He was just funny.

One night, we had friends over, like we often did. We were sitting around talking and one of our friends was pregnant and ready to deliver at any time. Like women often do, we started talking about our own birthing stories while the guys listened and pretended like they were interested. At some point, Chad decided to tell us the story, as he remembers it, from when our daughter was born. Now, listen, I think I do a good job of telling stories in a comical way. But, I can't come close to how he told this story that night. He told it four different ways in a ten-minute period and we laughed so hard that I am not ashamed to admit that I peed my pants a little bit, and my friend almost went into labor. The story itself was funny, but by itself not that hilarious that my stomach should hurt for days on end from laughing. It was the *way* he told it. The *way* his voice inflected and the laughs he inserted. The way he recounted the time when our daughter was born, and he had to put on scrubs to be in the operating room and how he didn't know they were paper and thought he had to take off all his clothes to wear them. About how he realized that he should have left his clothes on, but it was too late because the baby was being born, yet his scrubs were ripping in places they shouldn't and chafing him. About how he was scared to move too much or he too, would have been in his birthday suit. I still giggle when the moment catches me, but at the same time, I am frustrated because I can't remember it fully. I should have recorded him. I should have tried to memorize it. Because now, I have forgotten how he sounded, how he looked, how he made us laugh.

Last year, I found some audio recordings of him. They weren't about anything. They were more technical than anything else, but as I listened, I could still get a glimpse of what he was like. I could still remember little bits and pieces. But, my memory will not work the way I want it to anymore.

I think that is the hardest part of loss. The hardest part of death. The cruel reality. We start to forget. Our memories become blurred. The sounds fade.

I am not just forgetting what he sounds like. I am forgetting what he smelled like and what he felt like. I am forgetting the pattern of his breathing. I am forgetting the exact shade of blue in his eyes. I am forgetting the tone in his voice when he told a joke. I am forgetting how it felt when I laid on his lap and he pet my hair. I am forgetting what his hands looked like. I don't have any pictures of his hands. I am forgetting what the leather sounded like on his police belt when he put it on to go work, and what the Velcro straps sounded like when he took it off. I am forgetting how the stubble on his face felt when he didn't shave for a day. I am forgetting how strong he was. I am forgetting how he made me laugh when I saw him doing something silly. I am forgetting what the muscles in his forearms felt like. I am forgetting what his face looked like when he would give me a look after I did something silly. I am forgetting what his ears looked like. I never thought to memorize what his ears looked like.

I still sometimes catch myself thinking, "Oh, I will have to ask Chad about that when he gets home." Sometimes, I forget that he is gone.

It's the strangest feeling to feel like they are still coming home but at the same time you can't remember what they sound like.

We talk about him. We remember him. We do our best to honor him. But, we still forget.

Not long ago, my teenager got in trouble and I was trying to figure out what to do. I wanted her punishment to be fair, but I also wanted it to be consistent with what Chad would have done. I often find myself asking that question, "what would chad do?" to the point where I joked about getting wristbands made and starting the hashtag: #WWCD. I want her to be parented the way we had planned. The way we decided. We wanted certain things for her and we wanted her raised a certain way, but when he died, she was 13. We were parenting her as a 13-year-old and not as a young adult. I don't know what I am supposed to do half the time. So, I did the only thing I could think of and asked my kids what they think Chad would have done in this situation. Their responses were perfect. One, of course, was something like, "I dunno, what did gramma do to you?", one said they were "too afraid of him to find out" and the third said he would have "grounded her and taken away her car." Nothing too crazy, nothing too dissimilar than I thought they would say but it was during these conversations and, subsequently, discipling my daughter that I figured out that Chad might be gone, and I might be forgetting things, but there are some things I will never forget. I will never forget the values and morals that he was built on, or the lessons or ideas that he taught us. That will never go away. His legend is just that. The ideas and lessons he left behind that I will impart to his children and they will impart to theirs and so on will ensure that his legend lives on. Generations will be affected by him. Children who he will not know will do things or make decisions because of the lessons he gave to one person who passed it down forever.

So, yes, I am forgetting what he sounds like, and how he felt and the inflection in his voice, but I know that there will always be a part of him in me, his children and for lifetimes to come.

But, in the saddest moments, and the darkest nights, I can't help but refer back to a message I received after he died. This was from my friend, Wangui Mbatia Nyauma, from Africa, who had the same cancer Chad had. She was the most eloquent wordsmith I have ever spoken to, and I would like to share her words with you. I hope it brings you the same peace it did for me.

"Diana Lynne Register, my heart aches for your loss. Yet, at this time, I can think only of the words that came to my mind when my father passed away; that if a man's greatness is to be measured, it is best measured by the quality of the life he lived,

which is best indicated by the family he leaves behind.

I know Chad only through your eyes, through your love. Yet I know you through the same love, for it is by your actions at the hardest of time that your greatness is apparent. You and Chad = greatness.

I am not qualified to talk but having walked the road that Chad walked for some time now, I can tell you that there is nothing more valuable than the friendship, the love, the laughter, the romance of a best friend... nothing is a better antidote for pain than that. That's what you were for Chad, and for that, you are special.

This will not be easy. It will hurt like hell. There will be moments of despair, when you want to have him back, just for a moment, for a flash of his smile, a scent... the echo of his laughter. I'll tell you what I would want my husband to know... that great love is everlasting. It is forever. It changes, yes, but it lasts. The life you have shared will be, the memories will last, and there's Kaitlyn... that wonderful bond, that perfect union.

I am so sorry that you are going through this without the love of your life to hold you still-physically. In the silence of the night, when all is quiet and the sky sparkles with the stars... if you listen to your heart, you will know that he is there yet.

I send you lots of love. In Africa we grieve by talking, by remembering the things we shared with a person. It makes us wordy. In remembering through words, we always invariably end up in a celebration.

So, I celebrate Chad's life, it was a life well lived. I celebrate you, I celebrate Kaitlyn- you who held him tight and sent him off the way every man and father should go - in the arms of the people he loves and who love him back unconditionally. I

94

celebrate your bond, I celebrate the bond that glues you together, the bond that is not broken by death.

I thank God who saw it fit to put a unique, yet perfect, family together. I trust that the same God has you in his arms, Diana Lynne Register that his plan is to prosper you, even now, when things look bleak.

Thank you, James "Chad" Register, legends like you live on in many different ways.

Fare thee well, to the land of ceaseless peace where the sun shines softly, the rains never lack, and the grass is always green- the land where love never stops."

The Firsts, Seconds, Thirds, Holidays and Beyond

"First, there is no typical grief cycle, and second, it's not something I went through. I am still grieving." Tony Dungy

There is a fallout from death. A fallout that extends beyond the first year.

I love the people for being there for the firsts. For the first holidays, the first birthday, the first anniversary and for all those first painful moments and experiences that no person should have to bear alone. I am thankful for the cards, for the flowers, the notes, the texts, the calls and the thoughts. I am indebted for the prayers as we struggled through the first of everything without him. I am honored so many people helped me survive.

Now, to those people:

Go back to your lives. Do the things that bring you happiness. Search out your passions and grab them. Love hard and love often. Take chances.

Wish on dandelions and falling stars and at 11:11. Breathe in the moments with the people you love and memorize their face, and their hands, and the sound of their voice. Work diligently, achieve your goals and then go home and forget them while you watch a movie you don't want to watch but you will because that person you love wants you to. Learn from my grief. Learn to appreciate the smallest of things and learn to forgive without reservation and love your people every single second like it might be your last chance. Yes, go live your life.

But please; please be there for the seconds. And the thirds. And every year after that. Because, we still need you. We are still lost.

My grief is not gone. My grief did not end when the first 365 days came and went. My grief is still raw. It is still painful. And it is still very present. It is still a fire that consumes my very bones.

The first few days after my husband died, everything was a blur. I woke up, I handled whatever I had to, and I went back to bed. The first few weeks after he died, I tried to figure out what normal was. I found that I hate the term "the new normal" because there is nothing normal about this. There is nothing in my life that is normal anymore. It's not a "new normal", it's a new, painful reality. The first year after his death, I went through the motions and just tried to live a life that was empty in so many ways.

I do my best now to fill it up; to fill up the crevices of myself that are numb with new things. New adventures. New purpose. New goals. New hobbies. New people. Yet nothing, nothing is "normal."

My husband is still gone. I still look for him in crowds. I still look for something, anything that I can hold that he once did. I still yearn for his jokes, for his smile, for his silly quirks. I long to hear him snore, a sound that I didn't love when he was alive, but one that would be a melodic masterpiece for me now. I ache to walk out into the kitchen to see the peanut butter he left out, lid off, with a knife placed on top. Something that was so irritating to me before he died, yet I would do anything, absolutely anything to see it again.

That hunger for him did not go away in the first year. It may have quieted a bit, but it has not gone away. Yet, in a strange way, it has been replaced with the 'what-if's,' instead of the searing pain of the sting of the first set of events.

In fact, as I write this, I wonder what I would be doing if he were alive. What if he was here? Would I be making dinner? Would I be dancing with him in the kitchen or laughing at one of his jokes? Would we be arguing over who was right about some silly thing? Would we be planning a vacation? Would we be passing each other in the hall, kissing goodbye as one of us left for work?

What if? What if I had pushed him to do more treatment? Something more aggressive for his cancer. What if I had talked to more doctors? What if I made him try some alternative medicine? What if?

It's not the fear of the firsts anymore that preoccupy us. It's the what-if's.

Because as time moves on, and the fog lifts ever so slightly and clarity enters my life, these are the things that haunt me now. And, I still need you to understand. I still need you to understand that I am tired. I still need you to understand that it is hard to find joy in some things. I need you to understand that my soul is exhausted whether my body is or not. I need you to understand that some things are still hard. I need you to understand I am terrified of my future; a future that was once so beautifully predictable is now so uncertain. I need you to understand that I am anxious, and I am worried, and I am regretful. I am full of guilt.

I feel guilty that I survived this tragedy, even though it was what he wanted me to do. I feel guilty that he died. I feel guilty that, at times, I am happy. I feel guilty that my kids don't have him anymore, because he was the better parent. He was the better person. He was just better.

Yes, there is a fallout from death. There is a fallout from grief. And, I don't know if it ever really goes away. I'm sure it changes, but the grieving person will never be the same. We will never be 'normal' again. We will be scarred, flawed and irrevocably different.

So, please, please don't forget us as we move on with our lives and you with yours. Please don't forget to show up when you can, reach out when you have a minute, and sit quietly with us in our grief, even if it's now different.

We might be OK some of the time. Heck, we might be OK most of the time. But we still need you. We still need you when the second birthday comes up. Or the second holiday. We really need you when the second anniversary comes up because we need the distraction. Because as the second, third, fourth, fifth anniversary rolls around, it will always seem like the first.

So, thank you for being there. Thank you for loving us and being patient as we figure out the process. Thank you for standing by us in the first year.

But please, don't forget us in the second.

~*~

I am sure we are all in different places in our grief. Some of us are just starting the process. Some are a year in, some two, some three, some four and beyond. What I have found as I collect the years, that it never just goes away. It never just gets easier. There's not a magic date where suddenly the pain is just gone. I dare to say that the first year is probably the easiest, as weird as that sounds. Mostly because I think you're in a fog. I heard grieving people use that term before I lost Chad, but I don't think I really understood what that fog was like. You're tired. Confused. Numb. Paralyzed at times. But that fog is also a weird blessing. It's like anesthesia. You don't feel hardly anything. And some of what you do, you forget. I promise you that some of what consumes your mind in the first year will ease. It's like looking at an old picture. When you first take it, it's vibrant, colorful, clear and sharp. And over time, it fades. The colors dim, lines run together, the picture might even get a little bit wrinkled or stained. It's not that you can't still see the picture the same way you did the day it was taken, you just don't see it as clearly as you once did. What that means for the grieving person is that the terror will ease. It will lose its color eventually. It doesn't totally go away, but it will start to fade.

After Chad died, I could not get the image of him taking his last breaths out of my head. If I focus now, I can still remember it vividly. The way it sounded, how it looked, how helpless we all felt. The confusion. The anxiety. I remember what his skin felt like as I held his hand. But, in the beginning, I could not talk about it without practically having a panic attack. As I write this today, my stomach hurts while I recount it, but it's not the same. At the time, it was a living nightmare and even when I was asleep, it would wake me up. I would gasp for air. I never thought that would go away. I remember a friend of mine telling me it "will go away". I wanted to punch him in the face. It never felt like it would get easier. But, it did, friends. It did. It still hurts but I don't feel like I am going to throw up anymore.

As we move into subsequent years, some things do get harder at first. People forget. They move on. The first Christmas after Chad died, so many people remembered. So many people showed up. So many people left gifts. It was great. I felt comforted. I was not alone. By the second one, people didn't show up as much. I didn't expect them to, to be honest, but I also wasn't totally prepared for the difference. I wasn't totally prepared to do it all on my own. I think people thought I was, but I wasn't. I still wanted people to come around. I still wanted somebody to sit with me by the fire and eat cookies with me. I still wanted somebody to drag me out of my house to build a snowman. I was still so lonely.

I think a lot about the grieving person when it comes to holidays. As I've said before, grief isn't reserved for people who have lost somebody to death. We're all living a 'grief life' in some ways, because we've all experienced loss somewhere in our lives. All of us. All of us have lost somebody even if it's in different ways; whether it's death, divorce or just the idea of what we thought something was. We have all experienced change in some form; the loss of a job, the home we grew up in, friends – anything that was important to us. We all carry this with us as we go on about our lives, and while some loss feels bigger than others, I think any loss produces the same grief process whether it's considered big or small. It's the same cycle. The same emotions.

In saying that, when the holidays come around, they act as a trigger, whether we want them to or not. There's always that 'before and after' feeling. For me, I identify with 'before Chad got cancer' and 'after Chad got cancer,' or 'before Chad died' and 'after Chad died.' There's that break in our lives. We all have it, it's just some of us have a break that is more noticeable or more pronounced. Either way, as we move along with our grief, we're all comparing our life to a degree between 'before' and 'after.'

Before Chad died, holidays were fun. They were creative. They brought together all of those feelings of family and tradition. We looked forward to them. I laugh when I think back about how badly our daughter Kaitlyn wanted a dog for Christmas one year and how badly we didn't want one. We had already had a stray rag doll cat run away after Kaitlyn decided it needed suntan lotion slathered all over it so as not to get sunburned, a fish that literally jumped out of the tank and died on the carpet, and a pigeon that took up residence in the garage and would not leave. The universe was clearly sending us signs that we were better as a no pet family; yet Chad, wanting to please his little girl, settled on buying her one of those pretend dogs that walked and barked and who knows what else. That was until she played with it, for exactly three days, and he looked at his receipt and realized how much he paid for an overpriced stuffed animal. Believe it or not, that pretend dog ripped a hole in his box and ran away by New Years, and Kaitlyn was none the wiser. I'm pretty sure the cashier at Costco, upon processing the return, was curious why there was a huge hole in the side of the box, but you know – ask no questions to the middle-aged man holding a ripped doggie box just trying to get his money back.

Or, the time when Kaitlyn tried to catch us being the Easter Bunny, yet thankfully we found her phone on the counter recording us in the kitchen before it was too late. How he managed to make a movie and place it on her phone, I have no idea. But when she woke up the next morning, she didn't see a recording of mom and dad hustling around putting together baskets or stressing out trying to make perfect bunny foot prints on the floor out of flour. No, she woke up to a video of the door opening, pushing in glitter (must've been a fan), the sounds of a bunny hopping throughout the house (something like 'boing, boing, boing'), lights flashing in the kitchen complete with music and then, suddenly, her Easter basket appeared on the counter.

Those are the things I miss. I miss how he managed to make everything alright when holiday stress was too much. I miss how he had this golden touch that made everything fun, how he knew what the perfect gift was, and how he managed to bring calm in any kind of chaos.

When he died, it wasn't just those things that changed. The whole atmosphere changed. The same thing happened after my step-dad died. It was like everything we knew for decades, every tradition we had, everything – was different. We tried to keep it up, but it was never the same.

After Chad died, I tried to make new traditions. We tried new things. But in the back of our minds, we always knew that the only thing we really wanted for the holidays was him. And that was something we would never be able to make happen.

The first Christmas Eve, the actual night, I spent it alone. I had to. I needed to. I didn't want to go to his family's house and play the white elephant gift game – you know the one where you bring something you don't want any more to give somebody else – and be reminded about the time he wrapped up the mortgage in a box because he didn't want it anymore. Or the time he threatened to take the real dog we eventually welcomed into our home. I didn't want to sit there and look around the room and know he was missing. I didn't want to jump every time the doorbell rang wondering if it was him and he was just late. I had to process it in my way, which turned out to be sitting in my closet with a bottle of wine. I was very lucky to have good friends who forced me to go Christmas shopping, so the kids could have stockings and treats, but was my heart in it? No. And, I'm not afraid to admit that.

It was hard. Holidays are hard. And so are Tuesdays at the grocery store buying stuff for dinner knowing there's one less person to feed.

It wasn't until Father's Day that I decided I had to step up and do something for my daughter that would help her heart heal. I googled things to do and was just not interested in releasing balloons in his honor or dedicating a star in his name. So, we made a list of things he loved and funny things he did, and we reenacted them in a video, with Kaitlyn playing him. A Costco trip for steak, a ride on a motorcycle, breakfast at Cracker Barrel, fishing on the banks of a creek, playing the guitar, sleeping with the dogs, sitting in a patrol car and the list goes on. We simply, and quietly, relived a day in his life. And it was fun. And it was goofy. And we laughed, a lot. Because even though we knew we couldn't have him back, we were never going to let go of him.

The holidays are going to roll around, and I wish I could tell you what the perfect way is to deal with them. I wish I had some amazing answer, or as my mom always says, 'I wish I had a magic wand to make this better.' I don't. But, what I do know is that however you manage to get through them will be the same way you get through Tuesdays at the store.

Sometimes, you will want to be surrounded by family and friends. Sometimes, you will want to sit quietly in your closet. Sometimes, you will figure out a new tradition, or maybe you'll take a vacation. But, no matter how you do it, you will find a way. Because, while your grief is there, you do not have to sit in it. You do not have to let it consume you, no matter how badly it feels like it is.

You will learn how to compartmentalize. You will learn how to put grief and your memories in a box and how to take them out when you need to and put them away when you don't. And you know what? It's ok to do that.

It's ok to feel bad sometimes. It's ok to cry. It's ok to yell and scream and be mad at the world. It's ok to feel like you don't know how to fix it. It's ok to be regretful. It's ok to be bitter. On a holiday, or any other day, it's ok not to be ok.

But, it's also ok to feel good. It's ok to be happy. It's ok to make new traditions and new memories and it's ok to be content in that. It's ok to move on. It really is. It's ok to have new moments, and it's ok to breathe those in and enjoy them. It's ok to feel like everything might go right. And, it's ok to be ok.

You will figure out this grief life as you go, I can promise you that. Give yourself a break. Do the holiday if you want to, and don't do it if you don't. The world will not spin off its axis if you choose to let it pass by.

But no matter what you do, or how hard it gets, or how overwhelming it seems, make one choice that will always be the right one.

Always, and I mean always choose *you.* Always choose what is right for you. And just because something is right this year might not be what is right next year or the year after that because as we grow and change in our grief, our lives and our choices will too.

But choosing you will always be the right thing, and the one choice you won't regret. I can promise you that.

In grief, best friends can become strangers, while strangers can become best friends

"When I was a boy and I would see scary things in the news, my mother would say to me, 'Look for the helpers. You will always find people who are helping.'" – Mr. Rogers

It's strange how grief brings people together, or absolutely tears them apart. There's a point where it seems that your best friends become strangers, and strangers become your best friends. I never thought it would happen to me, but it did. My friendship group during my husband's battle and after his death was very, very strong. It was solid. But, at some point in the process, it was shattered. At the time, it seemed it was so broken that it felt like the pieces could never be put back together, yet when it was, my new relationships were better than the ones I lost before. It didn't feel like it then, but it needed to happen. While painful, the shake-up was necessary

113

to put all the right players in place for a healthy healing process. Everybody had a role and at this point in that process, some roles needed to change. I can see that now. I would not have been able to heal if things were left the way they were. I didn't know it at the time, but certain people needed to come in and certain people needed to go. It was the only way I was going to heal and move forward. It was another grief gift.

Even though I realize this now, it was not easy getting to this point. Losing, gaining and shifting was an absolute gift, but it was hard. It was so hard. Painful, really. Sad. As if the loss of my husband wasn't enough, the loss compounded was awful. What I mean by that is dealing with one loss, and then adding more loss on top of it is very difficult to process. You don't really know anymore what you're mourning. Are you refocused in your grief to the new loss or still mourning the old loss? Or are you now dealing with all of it at once? The friendship I am writing about was a "win" for me in the middle of the biggest loss of my life. When I lost that friendship, it hurt more than what I would think was normal, because it was like reliving the same grief over again and ripping open the wound. It became clear later that this particular friend was not worth it and the things she did showed her true character and I was truly wrong about who she was. In clarity, I was able to see how unhealthy that relationship was, but at the time, I couldn't wrap my brain around it. It was just pure confusion. How could somebody who had been there for me and offered so much support turn out like this? After all, she had this reputation of being so kind, generous and Christian-like, so it must be me, right? It could not possibly be because she was not the person she said she was. No.

I thought I had done something wrong.

I thought it was all me.

I thought I was a bad person.

I thought I wasn't grateful or appreciative enough.

Those thoughts were the same thoughts I had after Chad died. When he died, I thought I did everything wrong. I didn't do the right things. I wasn't good enough for him. I didn't support him enough. I didn't pray hard enough. I didn't find the right people to help him. It was all my fault.

But, the fact is, none of that is true, in either situation. I will admit – grieving people can be hard to deal with. We can be difficult. We can be irritable. We can seem unreasonable. We can decide that some silly point is the hill we're going to die on. We worry. We want to control something, *anything,* if it means we won't feel so out of control. We want somebody to just understand. We want somebody who can just sit in silence with us. We want so badly for somebody to just "get it". This friend of mine wasn't "getting it." I spent so much time trying to convince her of what I needed that I lost sight of the fact that she just didn't want to give it.

When I let go, the most amazing thing happened. Losing her brought the right people into my life exactly when I needed them. Removing her removed the wall that was keeping other people out. As soon as I was free, those people who had always wanted to be there but couldn't started to come in. And it was glorious. They came in and offered me things she couldn't – the freedom to be who I am, to not be judged, and they loved me without conditions, without demands and without trying to control my life. I could breathe again. I was comforted. It was peaceful. Finally, it was peaceful.

After my husband's death, I needed somebody to come in and take control. I am not afraid to admit that. I needed somebody to just come in and tell me to "sit there", "eat this", "call this person", "go here." I was in such a fog that I needed somebody to organize me. She did that for me. It served its purpose. But, as my life moved forward, and things changed, I needed to be able to move forward and change as well. And when it became clear that she could now allow me to heal in the way that was healthiest for me and my family, cutting ties

117

with her was the best thing that could have happened. Because, in the middle of this, another woman came along who didn't just see the truth in that situation, but immediately knew how to comfort me in my grief in a completely different way. She didn't want to control me through it. She wanted to love me through it. Through that, our souls connected, and our hearts intertwined. She reads my mind. She shows up. We talk. We cry. We laugh. We support each other. She's a second mom to my daughter. She loves my dogs (I think). She holds my hand and sits with me in my grief. I do my best to sit with her in hers. She braids my hair. She tells me my outfits look good. We do dumb things. Silly, laughable, girly things. And had the break-up of that other friendship not happened, I would have missed it. I would have missed out on this beautiful, loving, sweet, graceful soul sister of mine. *That* would have been the bigger loss. So, for that, I am grateful that my other friend saw it fit to leave.

Grief is tricky, but crisis is scary, and I think this is where everybody who has suffered any kind of loss can relate on some level. Generally speaking, losing something is losing some sense of security. You get divorced, it's scary. You lose your job, it's scary. You realize somebody isn't who you thought they were, it's scary. You lose somebody you love, it's scary. In fact, all of that is terrifying. You suddenly don't know what to do. Your role in life is no longer defined because your life is no longer how you knew it. In an instant, everything has changed.

When your loss is death, people show up. They instinctively show up. They bring food. They bring flowers. Cards. And you smile and thank them because you really are appreciative, but what you really need is somebody to show up with a blanket and sit on the couch with you and ask you to show them pictures of that person you lost. You need them to take you to the grocery store because you can't do it on your own in that moment. You need them to go with you to get your nails done and laugh at your dumb jokes. You need your hair lady to pour you a glass of wine when she does your hair because she knows you just need to relax. You need your friends to tell you they will take care of your dogs and let you sleep in their guest room without question. You need them to ask you for the old stories because they know how badly you want to tell them. They know how much those memories fill up your entire body and sting your heart so bad that you have to get them out. They know you want to say their name out loud. They know you have to talk about them and who they were, and not just about your grief. They know you have to express how much you love them, even if it's only your tears that can speak. They know you have to smile. They know they have to check on you at random moments in the day so that you will know you're not alone. And sometimes, all of those needs are filled by the beauty and wisdom of a stranger. I was so lucky to have that. It impacted me more than I can even express, and it came to me without even asking for it.

But, what if it doesn't? What if it doesn't just come?

You ask for it.

I know how hard this concept is, especially when you're grieving. So many of us are hard wired not to ask for help, but sometimes, it is absolutely necessary. The phone feels like it weighs a million pounds, I get it. But, you will be surprised at the reception you receive when you finally ask. And if it doesn't happen with the first phone call, or the second, it will happen with the third. People want to help. They want to be there. But, they don't know how. Maybe you don't know what you need from them, either, but maybe you just need them to come sit with you on the couch. Or take you shopping and end up with a dance party on aisle 5. It's ok to ask them for those things. It's ok to write a list of the things you need and ask for it. It's ok to tell one trusted friend what you need and have them rally the troops. It's ok not to be strong. Read that again. *It's ok not to be strong.* It's ok to rely on the kindness of

121

other people. People will listen. They will talk with you. They will dance with you. If they won't, then it's time to look for new people, but you have to get rid of the wrong ones first.

When Chad was really sick, I had to call for help. It was the hardest thing I ever had to do. Some of it was because I did not want to accept that he was really that sick, but part of it was because he did not want me to call.

Chad never missed work. Ever. In fact, before his diagnosis, he had not called in sick for seven years, and only left work long enough to have surgery out of state. He didn't call in sick for chemo. He didn't call in sick when his cancer came back. He didn't call in sick when the cancer moved throughout his body. So, when he came home early from work one night because he couldn't handle the pain, I knew something was terribly wrong. I wanted so badly to be wrong, but I knew. He knew.

Within weeks, his condition got worse. And worse. And worse. We were doing our best to keep up, but it was consuming him. It was literal chaos. Bewildering.

We were in and out of the ER trying to manage the pain, and somewhere along the way, he had a stroke. We had no idea. He mentioned his vision was blurry, but he was the kind of person who compensated so quickly for something that I had no idea how bad it was. I don't know if he did and just wasn't complaining, but I had no clue that he was suffering so bad.

The tumors had finally taken over his body and the pain became so bad that he could barely stand it anymore. The effects of the stroke were finally starting to show, and I felt completely helpless. I didn't know what to do. It all happened so fast.

One night, his pain took total control. He could not bear it anymore. He sat on the bed, a shell of his former self, overcome with agony. We would find out later that the tumors were in every organ, but also in his bones and a tumor was blocking his intestines. They said it was comparable to being in active labor 24/7.

I told him I had to call an ambulance and he refused. He did not want to go to the hospital. To him, "hospital" equaled "hospice" and he refused to go. He did not want to be sick and he did not want to die.

As strange as it sounds, I was so torn as to what to do. I knew he had to go but I was also trying to respect him and how he felt about it. I was also trying to justify keeping him home, flashing back to just a few days before when he was feeling better. Maybe he just needed a pain pill. Maybe a heating pad. Maybe if he just sat up, or laid down, it would help. After all, there was no way the worst could be happening.

But, as he continued to ache, I couldn't stand by and wish for him to feel better. I told him again that I needed to call for an ambulance and, again, he said no. I told him we had to, and he asked me to give him "ten more minutes." I gave him "ten more minutes" for two hours. And, finally, I told him he couldn't do it anymore and he didn't have to hurt, and I was calling.

He looked me straight in the face and told me if I did, that he would never forgive me.

My heart broke. I *loved* this man. I mean, I really, really loved him. He was my entire life. He was my person. He was my everything. He was the keeper of my stories, my confidante, and the person I made memories with.

And he was going to die. And worse yet, he was going to die hating me.

Because I called. And as the phone rang, I consciously thought to myself that if the dispatcher who answers the phone is a jerk, I am going to lose it. I am a 9-1-1 police and fire dispatcher myself. I know we get busy. I know we have to separate ourselves from the calls, but I just knew that the person on the other line was going to dictate my entire night. Because I was on the edge of a breakdown, and how this person treated me was going to determine if I had one that night or not. I was already so tired of people *not* being able to help. I just needed somebody, *anybody* to help him.

When the dispatcher answered, I answered the questions. Name. Address. Phone number. And then he said, "My name is Jeff. Tell me exactly what happened."

"My husband has stage 4 pancreatic cancer. He recently had a stroke and is in a great amount of pain. The tumors are everywhere. In his arms, his legs, his back, his shoulders and down his spine."

No question. No follow up.

Jeff's voice changed. He wasn't robotic. He knew there was nothing he could do. But his voice changed. I can still hear it. It was surrounded in compassion. His tone was dripping in comfort. He didn't have to say, "I'm sorry" or "That's awful."

All he said was "Alright." But, there was something in the way he said it. That "alright" (to me) translated to - *"I feel your pain", "I am sorry your husband is suffering", "I am sorry your family*

126

Diana Register/Grief Life

*is going through this", "I hate this for you", "I wish
I could fix this", "I'm here for you"* all at the same
time. That small change in his voice told me
everything that he wanted to say and exuded
compassion. Something I so desperately needed at
that point.

Things that happen during a crisis are burned
into your memory. I've told you before, I remember
the look on the doctor's face when she told me he had
a tumor, I remember the tears from the nurse who
cared for him the night he died, and I remember the
sound of Jeff's voice.

Jeff didn't do anything grandiose that night.
He didn't save Chad's life. We didn't do CPR. We
didn't do first aid. But, while he talked to me and got
Chad help, Jeff was comforting. Reassuring. And by
doing that, he dictated my mindset which allowed me
to be clear headed, calm and able to better
communicate with the doctors when we got to the
hospital. That small, tiny inflection that, for a brief

moment, made everything alright. Sometimes it's not the big things. Sometimes, it's simple compassion.

I didn't want to call. I didn't want to ask for help. Chad didn't want me to ask for help. But I had to. I had to get us both help in that moment. And because of that simple phone call, Jeff and I are friends now. Good friends. Family. Maybe it was trauma bonding, I don't know. I thought I would try to avoid him because I was afraid it would bring up bad memories of a hard time, but in all actuality, seeing Jeff or talking to him just reminds me that yes - there is still goodness in the world. Goodness in people that comes when you least expect it.

You just have to ask for it.

And sometimes, you won't have to.

During my husband's cancer journey, I mentioned before that I found the most interesting places to cry where he, or anybody else wouldn't see me. The closet was a favorite. The shower. But when I wasn't home, it was parking lots that became an asphalt covered oasis. I found very early on that red lights didn't work well because people look around when they're stopped waiting for the light to turn

129

green. They'll catch you with mascara tears and while they won't say anything, there's that awkward moment where you lock eyes and you know they're secretly wondering what's wrong with you. And then there's that feeling you have after a tragedy where you don't care what somebody thinks of you but at the same time, you don't really want to have to explain anything.

So, parking lots became my go-to place. Big shopping centers worked best because the other people who were there were busy. They were on a mission to get inside or get out and get home, and not usually super interested in the girl sitting in the car screaming into her steering wheel.

One day, I was on my way somewhere and knew I needed to stop for coffee. I don't remember what the particular problem was at that moment but, like most days, I was overwhelmed. I was on the phone and talking it through, when the person on the other end of the line said something that struck me enough to lose it right there. I could barely catch my breath and the ugly crying started.

The problem was, I was stuck in the coffee line. At our local Dutch Brothers coffee house. The one place where all the workers are young, happy and jamming out to music.

And there was no way out. I was literally blocked in, so unless I wanted to back right up into the SUV behind me, I was about to be seen for the mess I really was.

As I approached the window as a middle-aged woman with my hair in a bun, and with my face wet from crying, I could barely speak. I was still listening to the person on the phone talk, and I had two choices. I could speed off or I could roll down the window.

I rolled down the window.

But I still couldn't speak.

The teenager who was supposed to take my order was known to me, only because I frequented the place often. She took one look at me and saw how

131

disheveled I was and said nothing. She just handed me my drink. A drink I didn't order because I couldn't even muster the words, but a drink she would know I wanted.

I tried to smile when I took it from her and drove away and finished my call. By this time, I had pulled into a parking stall and was trying to regain my composure. I reached for my iced coffee, and when I looked down in the cup holder, I saw it.

A pink straw, and the words "We love you" written around it.

Ugly crying again.

This girl barely knew me. I don't even think at the time she knew my story. All she knew was that at that moment, I was hurting. She couldn't fix it. We couldn't talk about it. She couldn't hug me. So, she used the only tool she had in that instance – a pen, and a pink straw.

She wanted me to know I wasn't alone. And that whatever trial I was going through, that there were people out there who cared about me. That regardless of knowing all the details, they cared anyway.

It wasn't just a straw and a message. It was a powerful symbol of how the smallest act of kindness can impact somebody's life.

I take that lesson with me wherever I go, and I retell that story to anybody who will listen. Because I want them —*no, I need them*— to know how powerful their actions can be to a person in pain.

I visit a different Dutch Brothers now and that girl with the pink straw has moved on with her life. I

133

don't know what she's doing now, but to me, she left a legacy. A legacy of kindness.

Every time I go to the new stand, I ask for a pink straw. Mostly because it reminds me that no matter how challenging my day is, or could be, that there is always somebody out there who cares. I don't think any of them knew the story when I asked. I'm pretty sure I was just 'that lady' who wanted a pink straw.

Until one day when I told Jake, the manager, the story.

And guess what?

He shared it with his crew. And the meaning of the pink straw rose up again. And now *this* group of baristas knows how easy it is to change somebody's day for the better with something so simple.

And since then, they have dived into my story, wanting to help me raise money and awareness for pancreatic cancer. Not because it's affected them personally. Not because they have experienced that tragedy. No. They're doing it because some girl in Idaho thought enough one day to be kind and now that story lives on and has evolved into something so much more.

And just a few months ago, Jake told me he had a surprise for me. When I asked him what it was, he presented me my iced drink, with a purple straw.

135

Why purple? Because it's the signature color of pancreatic cancer.

More ugly crying in line, thank you very much.

They don't even really have purple straws. But the ones they get every so often; they have my name on it. Because they want to show me they care. They want to show me they're doing something to honor my husband. They want to show me I'm not alone. They want to be part of the story. A story they're helping create.

We often think we have to do something big to make a difference. We think we have to spend a lot of money or do a grand act. We don't. Sometimes, it starts from holding somebody's hand, or being present in their grief, or offering a hug, or writing a note, or reaching out in some way. And sometimes, it starts with a pink straw.

There are still so many good people out there, friends, who are so willing to give you these grief gifts. But, you have to be willing to accept them. You cannot shut yourself off from the world and believe you have to sit in your pain by yourself. You have to be willing to open up with your story, whether to a counselor or a priest or a family member, or a friend or even a stranger. I will never forget the lady who I saw sitting on a hospital bench outside one of the many hospitals we went to for treatment. I walked past her the first time and caught her out of the corner of my eye, immediately noticing she was crying quietly. She was hunched over a bit with a hospital bracelet on her wrist. I almost kept walking, but something told me I *had to turn around.* So, I did. I turned around and said nothing to her as I sat down next to her. I don't even know if she noticed me until I hugged her. I wasn't sure what her reaction would be. After all, I was a stranger sitting down next to her invading her personal space. She didn't stop crying. She didn't speak. She hugged me back. To this day, I don't know what was wrong in her life. I don't care. She didn't tell me. My hug to her and her hug to me was the only thing that mattered in that moment.

We weren't best friends. I don't even know her name. But, we needed each other, and we did exactly what we were supposed to do, because it was the right thing. As you grieve, you will find those people. You might have to look for them, or they might just appear, but trust me on this one – let it happen. And if it doesn't, *ask for it.*

Crisis Chasers

"Be the same person privately, publicly and personally." Judah Smith

We have all heard the term "ambulance chasers" but do you know there are real people out there who are "crisis chasers?" I am not referring to people who come out of nowhere and really want to help, or people who have their hearts in the right place. I am talking about people who look for people in crisis and swoop in with the sole purpose of making themselves look good.

This chapter is not meant to create paranoia within your support group. And, while it's hard in grief, you have to be smart about who you let in and who you don't. At the time, I felt like I was. I can only look back now and reflect. I see now how important it is to be watchful and mindful of people's behavior. You will see it, eventually. It might be slight at first, but when you start noticing somebody who is defensive or quick to attack over something you did that might make *them* look bad, you might be dealing with a crisis chaser.

This is my story.

I mentioned before that at the time of Chad's death, my friendship group was strong. Very strong. There were people who were travelling the journey with me closely, and there were people who sat on the fringe but who came when I needed them. I was grateful for all of them, but when the crisis truly hit, and he died, I lost sight of who was really there to help me and my family, and who was there to promote their own agenda. It's almost impossible to tell, they're so good at what they do. But, when Chad died, I had a friend who decided that her role was going to be all encompassing in my life. At the time, I needed that. I needed somebody to come in and tell me what to do. I was in such a fog that it was impossible for me to figure things out. She really did help at first, or so I thought, but the minute we had a disagreement on something, it became abundantly

141

clear that her intentions were not what she said they were. The control, the manipulation and the deceit were hard to recognize, but when it became clear, it was devastating. Devastating to know that somebody whom I trusted and cared about really never cared about me.

It was a perfect storm, really. I am a promoter, and vocal about my appreciation. I am very public about it, and my husband's death was all over the news. And, that was exactly what she needed. So, when the walls came crashing down and the truths were seen, she said to me, "Nobody will ever believe you." She said this because she was masterful at creating her reputation and had many, many people believing she was a selfless, loving, caring, generous person. And while some of that may be true, instead of wanting to repair our relationship—a relationship she worked hard at molding—her concern was what other people would think, and not losing me. And, instead of trying to repair it, she quickly moved to the next crisis within her friend group and took control there.

That's when I knew. That's when I knew she was never really part of my crisis because she wanted to help long term. She just wanted to be part of the crisis for her own reasons. It was a very sad, but necessary revelation.

There's something about being on the inside of the story that makes them feel important. It's a high. They can control things. They're managing. Setting up meals. They want to be close to the story. They want to be the reference point. My relationship became undone because I changed, and when I stopped living my life in accordance with her demands, she could no longer control me. She could no longer tell me what I was doing right or wrong. She could no longer control the people who were coming in and out of my life. And the sad thing was that the catalyst for all of it was really very insignificant but because it was the first decision I made about my life without her input, it shocked her so much that she couldn't fake it anymore. She couldn't digest it. She couldn't allow me to be me because it wasn't in her plans. It wasn't in her playbook. And when it fell, it fell hard. She did her best to turn people against me, but, luckily, most saw what was happening and didn't allow her actions to defeat us.

So, how do you know? How do you know when you're dealing with somebody who just wants to help, or somebody who is just chasing your crisis?

1.   **It's artificial.** Something feels "off." It feels fake in some ways. You know the old adage, "if somebody is talking to you about other people, they're talking about you to other people?" She was good at that. She spent a lot of time talking about and judging other people, then blaming me with cute quips like, "Oh my gosh, you bring out the gossip in me." Somehow her gossiping was my fault? She later told me that she often had to tell people to "give me grace" when they wondered what was wrong with

me. Knowing her as I did, I am sure that was her veiled response, but what she was really saying was, "Yes, there is something really wrong with her." By building up the idea that there was something wrong with the way I was handling my grief, she was successfully making herself the hero. She was putting a wall up and controlling the information that was disseminated because I was having too hard of a time doing it. And by making me into this version she wanted, which was weak and off balance, she could then publicly wrap her arms around me giving off the false impression that she was "fixing it."

2. **They act as the Gate Keeper, controlling who comes in and who goes**. After all was said and done with this, I quickly found out that there were multiple people who wanted to come to me after Chad died and who wanted to be there with me in my pain, yet she had not allowed them. She often sent out group texts letting them know what was going on, and what she was doing to help. And when they asked what they could do, she insisted she

had it handled. She did not want people slipping by and taking that spot she was so desperately trying to fill. Why? Wouldn't a true friend want somebody to feel loved by a lot of people? Wouldn't a true friend want the grieving person to have outlets? What would be the purpose of controlling that unless that person wanted all the applause?

3.   **It feels like love. But it's not.** Yet, it's so hard to decipher between the two. The only way you know it isn't love is when it falls apart.

4.   **They have the perception of importance at the expense of something tragic.** They insert themselves into your tragedy because it makes them feel important. But what they don't realize is that everybody who surrounds you in tragedy is important. Everyone is significant. Everybody has a place and a role. In my case, she could not handle that. When I mentioned what somebody else did, or said, or sent me, or how they made me feel, she discounted it. She attacked it. I had another friend who wanted me to talk to some

people from her church (which was a different religion than hers) and when she found out, she told me they were "preying on me" because that's what "they do to widows." She was so adamant about it that she showed up at my house when they were there to purposely interfere in the meeting. I don't know if she really felt that way about them or couldn't stand the fact that somebody else was trying to help, but it was awkward to say the least. She could not let me find peace in my way. She could not and would not accept that the way I found peace could possibly be different than hers.

5.   **They document their sacrifice in your tragedy.** When things turned, she immediately sent me a list of all the things she had done for me, which included stating that there were things she did "behind the scenes" that I never knew about. She documented every single thing she had done for me, right down to making my daughter lunch on occasion. And when she was done reviewing the list of her good deeds, she basically demanded my

gratitude. The funny thing was she already had it. She could just never see it because she was to busy noting all the things I was doing wrong that were making her look bad.

6. **There is an expectation you don't know exists.** How could you? If it's your first round with a "crisis chaser" you really have no way of knowing.

7. **They do "big" things.** It's not about organizing a meal train. It's bigger than that. It's making huge statements that will get them noticed. Over the top things. You can feel the difference in the purity of somebody who wants to come sit with you and watch TV so you're not doing it alone, and somebody who is doing things that are newsworthy.

8. **They are always in the middle of the crisis: yours or others**. They get attention for rescuing and have built their reputation on it. This goes without saying. Again, when things came crashing down, she was more concerned about her reputation than she was the loss of our friendship.

And to this day, people still believe she is genuine. They still believe she has a pure heart. To each his own, but I really hope the next person she rescues sees it quicker than I did.

9.   **When you push back, they attack.** As we heal, we start to change. And when you start to change and become more independent, a true friend will love and support that. A "crisis chaser" feels threatened by it. So, they attack. Your character, your children's reputations – whatever they can dredge up. And then they need an audience. They need people to side with them. They need people to agree with them. In my case, it wasn't just my friends she tried to turn on me, it was my child. When that didn't work, the attacks got worse. Instead of talking to me directly, she decided it would be better to address all our issues, even private ones, with a group of people in the form of a group chat. It was humiliating to say the least. Yet, again, it was somehow my fault.

10.   **When the attack is done, they move on to the next crisis, leaving you to feel blindsided.** She moved on to her next crisis very quickly, and that person started giving her public accolades as well. It was a weird choice since I didn't know they were really friends before that but, regardless, she turned on her charm and I watched her do it again – swoop in and save the day. I could do nothing more than shake my head.

Let me be clear, there is a difference between this and "trauma bonding". Trauma bonding can propel your relationship into a deeper connection. Those are the people who can handle your crisis and expect nothing in return. Those are the people who sit with you in your grief and let you direct it, not the other way around. Those are the people who have experienced or are also experiencing some kind of trauma in their lives that connects you. But, they never use you for their own gain. They find comfort in you, and you find comfort in them. Not uncertainty or pain. Those are the people who genuinely want to support you in your healing and do not need to do grandiose acts to help you get there.

After all was said and done, I really had to reflect, and I will be honest, I was angry. I was angry because I really believed she was doing everything she was because she cared about me. At first, when I thought about things, everything felt tainted. Everything was dirty. And I remembered the night that Chad died, I invited her to come sit with me. I did that because I really thought she was going to be my person. I did that because I trusted her. I did that because I needed her. But, when the truth came out, I was angry that I let her experience that sacred moment with me. She shouldn't have agreed to be there. She shouldn't have stolen that from me.

But now, with time and distance, I can look back on it and realize that I can still have that moment and remove her from my memory bank. I can still have that painful memory of my husband without her in it. I learned how to weed her out. I am thankful for that.

I also learned in this process who my real friends were because they are still here. I don't know what she's doing now, but I assume she is still rescuing people. Still filling the lonely parts of her life with other people's tragedy. I suppose she has moved onto the next and will probably continue that cycle for her whole life. I assume she is still chasing the crisis.

She will go on with her life and people will continue to believe the façade of who she says she is. They will continue to believe the reputation she has built for herself. They will continue to believe she is genuine. I cannot let that bother me. I saw the truth and it was an awful, shocking reality because when you lose the idea of what you think something is, it can hurt just as bad as anything else. So, I had to decide. I had to decide if I wanted to let her actions ruin all the good that other people did for us and continue to do or if I wanted to let go, no matter how hard, and live my life with the right people in. I had to figure out if I wanted to sit in more grief or learn the lesson. I have let go of her and I am better for it.

I have learned the value of the good people who came after. I hope I have learned an even more valuable lesson, which was to be a good, honest, genuine person myself. And to make sure my intentions are pure. To make sure that I am loving all the right people for all the right reasons. If I walk away from this with those things intact, then I am grateful for the lesson. I am grateful for the challenge. I am grateful for the way it all worked out. I am grateful that I had the opportunity to figure out who was really in my corner and who was using me. Because now, as life goes on and I'm not living in a constant state of fog anymore, I am doing things to better myself like working on this book and the foundation. I could not have done that if I allowed her to hold me back. I could not have done any of it without the right people around me. I could not have succeeded while somebody was constantly trying to defeat me. I could not have survived being suffocated.

I have tried not to allow this situation to destroy my trust in people. So many people are good. So many people's intentions are right. So many people want to help because they just want to help. So many people are honest and kind and pure and not trying to use your situation for their own gain. But, if you ever find yourself in the clutches of somebody who is a "crisis chaser," I just want you to know that as scary as it is, you can move away from them and flourish. You can, and you will, figure it out on your own. I know it's scary. I know they have been controlling big parts of your life. I know they have made you feel like you can't do it without them. I know they have taken on so much of your burden that you can't possibly imagine how you will start dealing with it on your own. I know they have made you feel like it's your fault. I know they have manipulated your friends and people close to you. I know they have made you feel uneasy about how you trust. I know they have gas lighted you, given you lists on why you can't live without them and blackballed you to prove it. I know they have, over time, whispered your insecurities in your ear and slowly massaged your fear to the point where your felt crazy. I know they have torn you down while building themselves up and I know they have used your tragedy against you. I know they have had you rely on them so much that you don't know how you can do it without them.

You can. Just like any other abusive relationship, it may seem impossible now but I am living, breathing proof that you can, and you will, do this without them.

And you will succeed. You have already faced and survived some kind of great loss. You have already looked fear in the face and won. You have already survived. You have already been through the worst. I have clichés, but it's true when they say, "if you can survive that, you can survive anything." You can. You will. You are.

I want to be just like him

"Be kind whenever possible. It is always possible.
– Dalai Lama

I have sat here watching the cursor blink on a blank page for at least five minutes. My eyes are heavy today. My heart is sad. It's just one of those grief days, I guess. We all know it comes in waves. I guess today is just a hard day.

Yesterday was great. I had a good night's sleep. Plenty to eat. I am hydrated. But for some reason, I am still feeling so tired. Grief weighs a thousand pounds, and, some days, it is hard to carry.

I want to tell you I don't know why I am so down today, but I know exactly why. I just don't know how to express it. I am doubting my ability to find the right words to tell you what I am feeling. But I am going to try.

When my husband died of cancer, many people sent me well wishes. Sincere, heartfelt well

156

wishes for he was a good man. So many people reminisced about how kind Chad was. How generous. How decent. I had always known this, so you can imagine how my heart swelled with pride knowing that other people knew it, too.

One friend of his told me how he had given him a piece of lawn equipment when he didn't have one of his own. Another told me how he was always smiling and how, even when he was sick, he was always looking out for others.

Last night, a friend of his told me that during the course of their job as police officers, Chad was the first to arrive on scene where a woman was dying after an accident. Chad was dying, too. He knew he was. The cancer was slowly eating at every part of his body yet, when he arrived on scene that day, it was not the first thing on his mind. The first thing on his mind was cradling this woman as she died. A stranger holding a stranger while she took her last breath. A stranger who was also facing certain death, putting that aside to comfort a woman he did not know. A stranger who was able to put his own crisis aside to hold her in his arms, so she would not be afraid. A stranger who whispered to her, "you are not alone."

And, simpler than that – he fueled up his police car. On his last night at work, he was in so much pain he could not stand it anymore and he had to come home early. Customarily, the officers at his department share patrol cars, so on their last work day, they fuel and wash their cars, so it is ready for the next officer when he comes on shift. The last night Chad worked was not his last scheduled work day, but he knew he was never going back. He knew he would be taking off his vest and badge one last time, for the last time. And in his despair and his agonizing pain, he still managed to fuel and wash the car before he came home early that night, only to die three weeks later. But, like always, he did the right thing. He did the kind thing.

He's gone now but these lessons stick with me. Admitedly, I don't always do the kind thing. I don't know many people who do. It's hard sometimes. It's hard to be nice in a world full of mean people. It's hard to look past people's shortcomings. It's hard to put a smile on your face when you feel like the world is crashing down. It is hard to be kind when life isn't going right.

And when it gets really hard, I remember these stories. I remember how, as my husband suffered, he never let it block what was right. He never felt sorry for himself. He never sacrificed the man he was in spite of his anger, or fear, or confusion, or sadness. He was never blinded by his cancer or his situation.

He looked life straight in the face and decided to do the right thing, no matter what his circumstances. He made the decision to fuel the car. He made the decision to hold that woman until she died. He made the decision to be kind. No matter what, he decided.

I think we can all learn from this. I think we can all decide to do the right thing. I see bad decisions all day long, every day, in every single place. I see people cutting people off in traffic. I see people arguing about petty things to prove who's right. I see people being mean just to be mean. I see people talking down to each other. I see people holding anger because they are too proud to forgive. And sometimes, they will never get the chance.

I had nightmares last night. I imagined what it must have been like to be him. I imagined what it must have felt like to hold a dying person knowing my time was near. I imagined what it must have been like to fuel the car knowing it was the last time. And, I imagined what the conflict inside of him must have felt like to man up in his fear and do it anyway.

It's a simple choice to do the right thing. It's a simple choice to be kind. I want to be like him. I want to be that person. I want to do the right thing. I want to be kind. I hope you do, too.

Triggers

"No one ever told me that grief felt so much like fear." – C.S. Lewis

Dear Chad,

I haven't been to Costco in almost two years. That was *your* happy place. If you were ever missing for a long period of time, I knew where you were. You were at Costco. I think you liked seeing all the new gadgets that had come out; you liked looking at the televisions, the cameras, the electronics, but I also think you found some peace there. You were able to get out of your head for a little bit. Focus on something else. Stuff you liked. Remember when you wanted to buy my engagement ring from there and I thought you was certifiable? I mean, who buys an engagement ring at a warehouse store? Who knew you could buy something really brilliant and sparkly while you're picking up paper towels? *He did.*

Yes, I haven't been to Costco in two years. Why would I? There's no one to enjoy it with anymore. There's no need to go buy things in bulk anymore. There are no gadgets to go check out so I can run home and tell you about them. There's no reason to go there to buy your coffee, or your steaks, or your tubs of licorice. You're dead. There, I said it. *You're dead.*

The week before you died, you insisted, *absolutely insisted*, that I take you to the Apple store. You were having trouble with your laptop and wanted it replaced. I remember you standing on the other side of the store talking to the salesman, and that was the first time I caught a glimpse of how thin you had become. How very frail you were looking. You looked pale. I was afraid you were going to collapse. I tried to ignore it but at that very instant I realized you were really, really, really sick. I still would not allow myself to believe you were going to die, but I could not believe what I was seeing or have it make sense in my brain. You could do anything. You could fix anything. Why didn't you fix this? It goes without saying, I don't go to the Apple store, either.

No, I don't go to Costco. I don't go to the Apple store. I don't drive the same streets you did, I hate seeing white Toyota Pathfinders and BMW motorcycles. I don't make tater tot casserole anymore.

I can't. I can't invite the triggers into my life. Not right now. Much like a drug addict who can't frequent the places where they bought their drugs for fear of a relapse, I can't do certain things or go certain places because I might fall apart. And, I'm ok admitting that.

I don't know what a professional would tell me, but I imagine they would tell me to face it. At least, at some point. I'm not ready. But, I still sit here and wonder if avoiding those things is normal. Do other people just do it? Do other people think it's weird that I want to avoid it? Do other people avoid it, too?

The answer is "yes." Other people avoid things, too. They avoid family gatherings, holidays, stores, parties and pretty much anything that is going to trigger those feelings for them. Maybe it's just human nature, or maybe it's fear. I mentioned before that crisis is scary. Losing somebody is scary. Facing it over and over and over again is scary.

Many of us are just trying to figure out how to get through the day and inviting a memory in that could act as a trigger is something we instinctively fight off.

I have the pillow you were lying on when you died. It's in a bag and put away. I have the clothes that you were wearing. I don't want to take them out and look at them, but I feel some kind of weird comfort knowing they're there. The nurse folded up your t-shirt and put it into a Ziplock bag, so it would smell like you if I wanted it. I have never opened it, but I am glad I have it. As I write this, it almost sounds morbid, but it's not. People who have lost somebody they love will hang onto just about anything if it means they are close. I don't know what will happen if I take those things out and look at them or touch them. I'm not ready to find out. Two years later, and I am still not ready. Your clothes are boxed up in the garage, but I can't get rid of them. A pair of your shoes are in my closet and I am not ready to move them. I don't know when I will be. I have decided not to assign a timeline to it. Some people are ready to get rid of everything right away, and some people aren't. Some people are ready to face their triggers and some people aren't. Like I said before, there is no right or wrong way to grieve. I will do it when I'm ready, and so will they.

I want people to not fault yourself if they are moving faster or slower than somebody else. This is their journey. Their process. Their story. Nobody gets to write it for them.

And, nobody gets to write mine.

Love, Me.

Winks

"To love is to receive a glimpse from heaven" –
Karen Sunde

When I write, I listen to music. I try to drown out the sounds that surround me. Right now, it's the wind. The dogs coming in and out of the doggy door. Beeping sounds from the kitchen; I'm just trying to ignore it and hope nothing is actually on fire. I sat down in front of the computer and it happened. "Right down the Line" by Gerry Rafferty popped up on my play list. I can't imagine any other song coming on right now because, when Chad and I got married, he made me a mix CD (yes, we still did that), and this was the first song on it. And here it is, coming up again when I need it the most.

I look for signs. I look for winks. I look for anything to show me he's around. I had known Chad for almost my whole life and having him gone for eternity just is impossible to comprehend. I hear

167

people say, "He's watching over you," or "He's still here," but how do we really know that?

For me, I've been lucky. I don't know what other word to use, except lucky. The signs he has sent me have been comforting. Funny. Everything I expect from him.

Now, in saying all of that, can I reach for signs sometimes? Yes. Can I see something and try to make it a wink from him? Yes. But most of the time, it hits out of nowhere and actually takes my breath away.

The first sign I ever received was the week after he died. My mom lives in Southern California in the home we grew up in. It was built in 1923-ish and has that charm and beauty you would expect from an old house that's been kept up throughout the years. The ceiling in the living room has exposed beam, most rooms have hints of or full hardwood floors, and the property sits on about a ½ acre which is huge for this area. It's long and narrow and extends back about a whole city block. It's full of flowers and trees and grass and a pool, a guest house, privacy and sweet memories. The house is surrounded by windows, all of them open with a latch causing a cross breeze throughout the house.

If you've never experienced a California summer, I'll give you the highlights. It's warm. Sometimes super-hot. But most days, the early mornings are cool, it warms up throughout the day, and piques between like noon – 3pm. It starts to slowly wean off and by six or so, it cools off again but it's still warm. Warm enough to be outside with a tank top on, but cool enough for a light sweater.

Ok, so now that we have that established, summer was a favorite for Chad and me. We met in May 1988 and spent the summer driving around with the sunroof open, doing anything outside, and hanging out all night with friends after the carnival at Victory Park. But our favorite place to go was Eaton Canyon at night, mostly because we weren't supposed to be there, I guess. Oh, how I loved those warm summer nights sitting on top of the picnic tables, breathing in the scent of the oak trees scanning for falling stars. I drove past there when I visited after he died. It's different now. Whether it's really different or just different in my brain, or maybe because it looks totally different in the daytime, I don't know. I didn't stick around long enough to really explore. I wanted to see it, but I'm not sure my heart was ready.

Maybe it was all the chaos that triggered the nightmares. Maybe it was the memories. Maybe my brain just couldn't take it all in.

That night the first one happened. I was asleep in the front bedroom. There were windows on two walls of the room that were left open for the breeze. An old oak tree sits just outside the window and shadows the house. I fell asleep with the TV on and, sometime after that, I had a nightmare that I was awake, and in a panic. Sheer panic. I didn't know where I was or what I was doing. I was just panicking. I was trying to fix something, but I didn't know what it was. I was just scared. So scared. The next thing I knew, I was standing by the pool equipment and there was this weird, scary 'Halloween' looking guy setting things on fire. All I could think was that he was going to catch the pool equipment on fire and it was going to blow up. I remember screaming for Chad and telling him we had to run. I sprinted behind the pool and to the gate that would lead me out to the long driveway and back to the garage. I remember getting the gate open but that was it. I don't remember anything after that other than I was so scared and totally out of control.

The second night and the second nightmare – it was the same thing but different. It was just panic. Out of control panic. I again wanted to fix something, but I couldn't.

By the third night, I had had enough. I had barely slept in a month and couldn't handle another night of terror.

So, I asked him. Out loud. I asked him to help me. It sounds crazy, but we were only a couple of weeks out from his death and for fifteen years he was the one who took care of everything, especially me. I didn't know what else to do. My brain wasn't trained yet not to ask him for help, because he was my person. My go-to person anytime I needed something. He knew everything about me. He knew how to fix everything, calm every fear and stop all of my anxiety. If he had been alive, I would have told him about the nightmares. He would have said something magnificent to put my mind at ease. At that moment, I just didn't care if he was standing in front of me or lingering around in the air, I asked him.

And that night, I fell asleep again with the TV on and the windows open. At about 3am, I woke up with nothing on my mind. Nothing. No fear, no panic, no crazy dream. Just this indescribable calm. The breeze was slightly coming into the room, and the moon was as big as I have ever seen it. It was so bright that it shone right through the old oak tree and into the room. Even the scent of the air was different, like a subtle hint of fresh cut roses yet I knew there were none around me. The temperature was perfect, not too hot and not too cold. I wish I had the appropriate words to describe what it all felt like, but I don't. Because it was something so incredible that I don't think the English language has even developed the words yet. Everything was undeniably perfect. So perfect that I pulled the covers up slightly and fell right back to sleep. A deep, wonderous, calm, peaceful sleep. No tears, no sadness. Just peace.

And, as insane as it sounds, that's how I knew he was never going to go far away.

Chad was charged with taking care of me, and he did it well. When he died, I had to figure out things like who our mortgage was through. Credit card debt. How to pay the cell phone bill. It's not that I'm incompetent, it's just that he did all those things. He was so good at being organized, responsible and grounded. It wasn't easy.

Before he got sick, we used to joke about ghosts and spirits and stuff and he didn't believe in it. I did. He would make fun of me and taunt me with things like Ouija boards. He knew I was scared of them, so every now and then one would show up. And it wasn't just me he terrorized them with. There was an officer at work who was as scared of them as I was, and Chad would make them out of paper and leave them on his computer. One night, he brought a Ouija board home and dangled it in front of me like somebody would a mouse or something, and I demanded he keep it in the garage or throw it away. He laughed, and I don't know what he did with it, but I eventually threw it away later that night and told him never to bring one of those things back into my house. The next day, I was sitting outside on the back patio and what do you think I found when I looked up at the back side of the patio table umbrella? Yep. The Ouija board nestled into the wires that held up the umbrella, in such a way it was staring back at me. After I threatened to burn the house down, he took it and I never saw it again. I don't know what he did with it, but I'm sure hoping it ended up in a landfill instead of on his partner's desk.

Anyway, this prompted a whole conversation about the afterlife, and I told him that if anything ever happened to me, I was going to come back and prove to him that spirits can come around. He laughed and finally agreed to do the same. He said, "Okay, Okay, if it's really true, I'll come back and show you, too."

And boy, has he been showing me. It started with the dreams, but then it got real. No matter how much I believed in it, I was still hesitant. But it got to a point where I couldn't deny it anymore. There was no explanation to what was happening.

The first big one happened after I had a date. Because, yes, that happens. Even the grieving date, but that's a whole other chapter so hang onto your hats and I'll get to that, too. I was very nervous about going on a date after some sixteen years of not dating, but there was something inside of me that decided I needed to try. Maybe I wouldn't fall in love or be whisked off my feet, but I needed to see what was out there. I was married to a man who was perfect for me in every way and I wanted to see if

175

there was anybody out there who I could even have a conversation with. After the date, he walked me to my car, which was parked in front of his house, in a circular driveway. The driveway was very long and spanned quite a distance. In my purse, I had five wristbands that I got from Chad's work, that were part of a fundraiser for his medical care. They are black, with blue writing, reading, "One Forty-Nine" on one side, and "CPD Calvary" on the other. 149 was Chad's police badge number, and "CPD" was short for Caldwell Police Department, where he spent his police career. The interesting thing about this was that those bands had fallen out of my purse a few days prior, so I tied them together and put them in the center pouch and zipped it shut.

The next day, my date texted me and asked me if I wanted to know what he found that next morning on his driveway. Of course, I did, but I was a little nervous. I was pretty sure it wasn't a tampon because I had a hysterectomy the year prior, so I was safe there. But, what was it? My ID? Credit Card? Some personal note?

Nope. This.

I had to take a double take, and of course my first thought was that it fell out of my purse. Or off my wrist. I immediately checked. The one on my wrist – still there. The five in my purse? Still zipped up and tied together. Maybe I had a random one in my car that fell out when I opened the door? I asked him where he found it. He told me. In a spot I never was. Even then, I had trouble believing it. Was it really possible? Could it really be? And if it was true, what was he trying to say? I remember the conversation with the date when he asked me if he could wear it to show his respect. I told him he could. He asked me if he thought it was safe. I quipped, "Well, I guess if you put it on and burn up, you'll know." He didn't burn up. But he did get his first ticket in twenty years a couple of weeks later. I guess Chad wanted him to know he was watching. Ha!

After that, we started working on the "#iam149" foundation. It all revolves around pancreatic cancer research and awareness and giving back to patients in honor of Chad's generosity. We created a video for pancreatic cancer awareness month and titled it, "I am 149", which basically showed how we were all in this together. We're all fighting a battle, and we're all going to survive in some way. That movement was born, and while people will tell you Chad was very private, which he was, he also told me that after he died, I could do whatever I wanted to use his story to help other people. So, I am. Because he deserved it.

The hashtag, "iam149" started showing up everywhere and it became synonymous with Chad and strength, fight and being a true warrior. Once it started moving around the country, I started getting the signs. Right when I needed them.

Our daughter, Kaitlyn, recently retired from competitive gymnastics. It's expensive. Like, really expensive. Tuition alone is equivalent to a car payment, then add in competition fees, leotards, warmups, travel expenses and so on. Every year, I was easily into it for at least $10,000 and the year after he died, she got invited to a competition that was going to cost roughly $400.00. In the grand scheme of things, it doesn't seem like much, but it was *another* $400.00. I didn't know how I was going to swing it, but when we found out, we happened to be in Las Vegas for another meet. Jokingly, I said I was going to throw down $20 on a slot machine and keep my fingers crossed. Just before that, though, we were walking through the hotel and the song, "Rise Up" by Andra Day came on the overhead speakers and believe it or not, that was another special song for him that became important to me after he died. I knew it was him. Just as much as I knew that the guy we ran into carrying a shih-tzu in the casino after the meet was meant to cross my path. Why? Because two weeks before he was diagnosed with pancreatic cancer, we were in Vegas for a gymnastics meet, and Chad told Kaitlyn that if she won, he would buy her a shih-tzu. And guess what? She did. And now, we have Karl, the black and white eternal puppy.

I took my twenty dollars and went on a mission to find the perfect machine. Chad was "old school," so I had to find an old school machine. Not a new computer animated one, but a real old school style Vegas one, complete with a pull-down handle and everything. I searched and searched and then there it was. Smack dab in the middle of the casino. I fed my twenty into it, closed my eyes and told Chad I needed his help with this one. We had to get Kaitlyn to Seattle to compete.

Pull one – nothing. Pull two – nothing. Pull three – nothing. Pull four, I finally hit something. It was small, but I clapped for myself anyway. And then, I noticed this:

Ok, so I blinked a few times to make sure I was seeing it right. I really, suddenly, had 149 credits? Really? Yes. Yes, I did. So, I pulled it again, and won. One thousand credits.

A few more pulls and I decided to cash out. How much did I win?

Exactly the amount I needed to pay for Kaitlyn's competition. Coincidence? No.

From that point on, Chad started showing up on money. I don't know why. Maybe he's trying to tell me something, but it's easy to find. You can't give me a dollar bill or a five-dollar bill without causing me to flip it over and check it fully, because if I didn't, I might miss this:

Or, this:

But one of my favorites was when he showed up for my other daughter, Savanna. Savanna is one of those kids who everybody wishes they had. She is smart, determined, dedicated and passionate about what she believes in. Sometimes, our views don't align. However, Chad and I wanted to raise her to be her own person, independent of us and we did our best to support her no matter if we agreed or not. We tried and tried to show her that, but I'm not sure if she totally believed it all the time. Until recently. She recently started attending USC and decided to participate in the Woman's March in Los Angeles. I don't know how Chad would have felt about it, but he showed up anyway. She was selling merchandise and taking money, and of course, he had to offer his support. Because it's what he would have done. He would have wanted her to know that even if he didn't understand or believe in the same things, it didn't matter. *He believed in her.* So, what did she find on one of the bills she took in for payment? Yes. He was there. As clear, and as wondrous as ever.

There have been more. So many more.

Last year, I was on my way to teach a class in Northern Idaho. The class revolves around him in some ways. As I was driving six hours to my destination, I thought about him. At one point, I started crying, wishing I was home with him instead and started questioning how I was going to do "this" without him. And by "this," I meant everything. Life. I turned the corner, saw it, passed it, then turned around and went back to make sure I wasn't imagining it. I wasn't.

I was going to Lewiston. He was with me. I don't know how else to explain it.

And sometimes, he's just being funny. Because he was *so funny.* He was a cop, so what was the meaning of this?

Remember the date I talked about earlier? He was at the gym recently and sent me this picture. He said that for as long as he can remember, this number has been missing. It took me a minute, but then I saw it. Even as bad as I am at math, I figured it out.

Yes. *149.*

Just this week, I have thought a lot about writing this book. I wasn't sure if it would be good enough, or eloquent enough or what people needed to hear. I sat down with a friend of mine for a cup of coffee, and we talked about it. She has a beautiful soul and her words resonated with me. The power of that conversation prompted me to get motivated to write. To share. To tell this story of grief and

189

survival and everything that happens in between. And, as I drove away with this new-found passion and commitment to this project, I thought to myself, "I really hope Chad is proud of me. Of us. I really hope this is what we're supposed to be doing." At the next red light, it became crystal clear. I pulled up behind this, saw it, and I knew I was on the right path. He might not be here to tell me with his words, but he certainly tells me with his signs.

I am forever thankful that I opened myself to receive the winks and that he sends them to me. I know a lot of people who will challenge this, who will say it's not real and it's all happenstance. They will say I was just in the right place at the right time, or that I'm just looking for them, so I have manifested it. The naysayers can say what they like,

I honestly don't care. Because real or not, it brings me peace. It brings me comfort. And in the end, that's all that matters. How we find "answers" is not for somebody else to judge. It's for us to enjoy. And boy, do I enjoy them.

Why?

"The question is not whether we will die, but how we will live." – Joan Borysenko

Dear Chad,

I guess this is the question of the century, for everybody. I never heard you ask this question out loud, but I can't imagine you didn't think about it once in a while. I know I did. I tried not to, but I couldn't help but wonder why you and not somebody else, or even why not me. You were the better person. You were the better parent. When I would ask this question, I knew there wasn't a good answer. We were never going to know why. We were never going to be able to justify that there was a "reason". There wasn't. There was no good reason this was happening. Your doctor said it was a fluke. That was our big answer. It wasn't anything you did. It wasn't some hereditary thing. *It was a fluke.* That was it. A stupid fluke. A fluke that took you away. I will

193

never understand that. I don't even know if I really want to understand it because then I might have to accept it. And I don't care that I'm supposed to go through some kind of steps that say I will get to acceptance. It's another way of saying there is some kind of closure, and you know what? There really isn't. I don't want to close this. I want to remember you. I want to keep you close. I don't want to let you go. The memories I have of you are not only associated with my grief, but rather, my grief is an extension of our life together.

The grief I feel is a result of the great love I have for you.

I say "have" because that will never go away. Ever. It will never be referred to in past tense. Somebody can give me the answers to all of my questions and it will still never change the outcome. It will still never make sense and there will still never be closure. There will never be closure because I am broken, Chad. I am irrevocably broken. I cannot be put back together. But, as I rise back from this fire that has consumed me, I will be alright. I want you to know that. I will just be different. From this point forward, my life is broken into two pieces. *Before Chad & After Chad.* So many of my sentences begin with, "Before Chad got sick" or "After Chad got sick" or "After Chad died." It's the new reality. People will say it's a "new normal", but I hate that term. There is nothing normal about this. Not one thing. I wish people would stop saying that. I don't know who coined the phrase, but it is not normal. It's a painful, awful reality.

You were not just my husband, or the father to my children, or my lover or my friend. You were my person. You knew every story. You knew every look I had. You knew my moods. You knew when I was up. You knew when I was down. You knew when I needed chocolate, or when I needed a coffee. You knew how to calm my fears. You knew when to talk, and when not to. You knew when I needed a break. You knew when I didn't want your help. You knew what every, single one of my sighs meant. You knew what tone I was using in text. You knew when my smile meant I was happy, and when my smile meant I was up to something; usually some kind of surprise for you. You knew how to make me laugh, oh Chad, *you knew how to make me laugh.* You knew how to put me at ease. You knew how to love me.

You just knew.

I don't even know how to teach that to somebody else. Anybody else. Because you, my love, were my person.

You were supposed to take care of me. I was supposed to die first. The kids miss you. They liked you better. Don't laugh, it's true. They did. One of them even said they wished it was me that died instead of you. I know that's their pain talking, but sometimes, I think it would have been so much better because while I am trying, I am probably screwing it all up. I hate that we will never know what life would be like for the kids if you were here. It's so unfair that we don't. And I feel so guilty that it was you. I carry that so deep in my heart, but I feel so guilty that it was not me. The world needed you. It still does. I want you to come back. *Please, just come back.* Come back and tell me why.

Because until I hear it from you, it will never make sense to me.

And until I hear it from you, I just don't want to know.

Love,

Me

Shine, my love, Shine

"I will see you on the other side of the stars."

As you know, when Chad died, he was placed in a mausoleum. By doing so, I quickly found out there was really no place to leave flowers as the cemetery had decided not to allow vases on the front of their headstones. You can leave flowers on the ground, but they get picked up every week and whisked away. So, we would visit him and not really leave anything. Except the notes.

When somebody dies, and you go to visit their final resting place, you instinctively want to leave something behind. Flowers, gifts, cards – whatever it is, there's just the feeling that you want to do something to show them you were there. I don't know why. It just feels right.

One afternoon in the fall after he died, my entire house had a meltdown. I can't remember why, but it was just one of those days. I was crying, my daughter was crying, I even think the dogs were crying to be honest. Nothing was going right. Nothing felt right. Everything was just a mess. I sat down next to my daughter, and together, we just cried. I looked at her, wishing there was something I could do to fix her pain at that moment. I thought about ice cream. Maybe a movie. Maybe she wanted a friend to come over. But the only thing I could muster through my tears was the simple question, "Do you want to go see your dad?" With her eyes swollen and her cheeks puffy from crying, she nodded. We left everything as it was and hopped into the car and started on the 30-minute drive to the cemetery. We didn't say much to each other, we just drove. As fast as legally possible, we just drove. We just wanted to be with him.

We pulled into the beautiful, tree lined cemetery and drove past the old headstones until we made our way to the mausoleum that housed my sweet husband. We quietly got out of the car and sat in front of him, still crying, placing our hands on the stone trying to touch him. I wanted to scream, 'come out of there right now,' but I knew it would do no good. So, we just sat, reflected and consoled each other while our hearts broke not knowing they could break any more than they already were.

As we got up to leave, it struck me that once again, we didn't have anything to leave behind. Just the tear stained concrete in front of his tomb, and parts of our souls.

We hugged each other as we walked back to the car and as she opened the door, there it was.

Two vials of glitter.

I laughed. I laughed a lot. Because, you see, glitter meant something to us and it is no coincidence it showed up in that very moment, right when we needed it.

At the time, my daughter was a competitive gymnast. She lived and breathed gymnastics and competed all over the West. They didn't allow the girls to wear nail polish or lots of make up during competitions, but they did allow them to wear glitter in their hair. So, we stocked up on spray glitter, and each time before competition, she and I would stand outside on the porch and spray glitter in her hair. I don't know if it was the first or second time we did it, but I remember getting a phone call from Chad one time after he had gone to work and he asked why there was glitter all over his work bag.

Imagine this for a minute. My husband was a cop. And sometimes he had to work on competition days, especially after he got sick and ran out of sick time. Unbeknownst to us, the glitter we sprayed on her hair would fall off everywhere, yet instead of ending up all over the house, it was ending up in his work bag. All over his jacket, his handcuffs, ticket book and on his shirt when she hugged him goodbye. And nobody noticed until he got to work and sparkled in the sunlight on a traffic stop.

I imagine that was a sight to see. A big, strong cop out there enforcing the law, covered in glitter and twinkling the whole time. He probably hated it. It probably bugged him. The guys probably made fun of him. But, guess what? He kept hugging her when he left the house, competition day or not. Glitter or not. Sparkly traffic stops or not.

So, on this particular day at the cemetery, when we saw the glitter as she opened the car door, we knew we couldn't pass it up. We finally knew what we were leaving behind during our visits. It was our thing. Our silly family thing. And I don't doubt for one second, he put it there to make sure we knew he was sending her a hug. So, we sent him a hug right back.

I bet he secretly likes it. I bet he's smiling. I bet he thinks it's funny. And I bet he's telling all his friends in Heaven the story about the time he was covered in glitter while writing a ticket in the sun.

It's hard sometimes to find the right way to honor your loved ones. It's hard to figure out the best way to show them and the world how much you loved them. Keep your eyes open, friends. It will come to you. I promise. It will come. It might be when you least expect it, in the middle of the worst day. And, it might come in the form of something you least expect, like a vial of glitter. *You just have to believe.*

I will embrace my love for you and show the world

"My body is my journal, and my tattoos are my story." – Johnny Depp

I let my 15-year-old daughter get a tattoo, and no, I don't care what anybody has to say about it. Documenting important events in the form of a tattoo is nothing new, in fact, some cultures still view it as an actual rite of passage. Warriors did it to commemorate their battles, and to honor those who have fallen.

I think the problem nowadays is anybody can walk into a tattoo parlor anywhere and get whatever fancies them at the time, which is great; until the meaning behind it loses its relevance. I'm pretty sure that most teenagers, and some adults, who are tattooing what's cool to them now won't love it forever and will eventually look at it with regret. So, when my teenager asked me for one, trust me, I thought about it. And thought about it. And thought about it.

What was her reason? What did she want? Was she trying to impress her friends? Was she just following some trend?

We talked about it and she told me that she wanted to get a very small, very appropriate tattoo to honor her dad, who passed away from cancer when she was 13. Even with that reasoning, I still struggled with it.

We talked about the tattoo her older sister, Savanna, got a couple of years ago. 'I IV IX' placed delicately on the top of her foot. For those of you that aren't up on your Roman numerals, that's 1-4-9, which was my husband's police badge number. I couldn't think of a more beautiful tribute. In fact, it still takes my breath away.

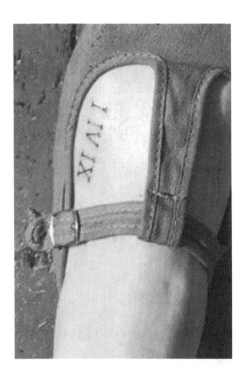

I started thinking about the meaning and it was so much deeper than just numbers. You see, after his valiant fight with his disease, his badge number has become synonymous with strength, courage and hope. That's what it means to me, and clearly what it means to my kids.

The night Chad passed, I told Kaitlyn she didn't have to go back into the room to watch him die. I told her I would stay in the hall with her. I explained what was happening, that he couldn't breathe, that there was a gurgling in his throat and it sounded like he needed to clear it but couldn't. I told her he would not wake up. I told her that he was going to stop breathing. And she didn't have to watch that.

She said nothing as she blew past me and straight to his bedside to hold his hand. She told the nurse she was going to throw up. Her body shook. Tears fell from her eyes. Her dad gasped. She sat straight up, wiped her face, swallowed hard, squeezed his hand and told him he could go. She told him it was ok.

She stayed with him while he died and didn't leave him for an hour after. She held his hand while he took his last breath, much in the same way that he held hers when she took her first.

In that moment, I knew she was her father's daughter. She was a beautiful example of the fighter he was.

After that night, she took a break from some things but returned to competitive gymnastics after a month and won the state championship for her age and level that year. She moved houses, made new friends, had plenty of girl drama, changed schools, and all the while got involved with pancreatic cancer awareness and research.

In the midst of all the change in her own life, she managed to continue to honor her dad.

And in my mind, that makes her a true warrior.

The things she has endured and the way she has survived is the true mark of all the things Chad was: strong, courageous and full of hope.

So, when Kaitlyn and her sister decided to get a tattoo to respect the battle and to honor their hero that fell, there was no way I was standing in the way of that. Not for one second.

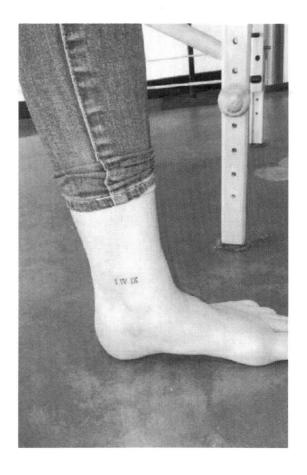

As for me, the day before he died, I asked for a copy of his EKG. I have his real heartbeat tattooed on my foot so every time I look down I know he's with me. It's part of him that is still alive.

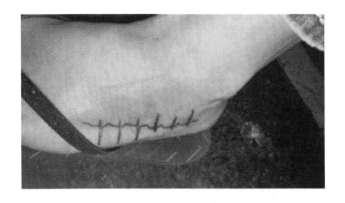

One of my favorite things was lying on his chest listening to his heartbeat, and now I can still see it anytime I want. And my kids can look at theirs and be reminded that they can survive anything.

So yes, I let my 15-year-old get a tattoo and no, I don't care what anybody has to say about it, because they have shown me, you, and anybody else who will listen what surviving looks like. They get to show that off however they damn well want to. They've earned it.

And, so have you. Nobody gets to judge you for how you grieve, and nobody gets to judge you for how you honor that grief or your person. When you start to feel overwhelmed by what somebody else thinks of you, remember, there is a fifteen-year-old girl walking around with a tattoo of her dad's badge number who is not bothered, not for one second, by the opinions of others.

If she doesn't, why would you?

I am afraid of my own mortality

"Death is terrifying because it so ordinary. It happens all the time." Susan Cheever

There is something really weighing on my mind. I guess it has been for a long time now, but it's really been on my mind lately and I can't shake it. Before Chad was diagnosed, I was always worried about my health. I had a lot of anxiety about it for some reason and always have. Maybe it relates to my fear of death. I wish I could remember where it started, or why I became so fearful of it. I don't, I just know it's always been there. I think it got worse during my pregnancies - just never knowing what was normal and what wasn't. Then having kids and worrying about them and their well-being. Constant worry. Constant fear that something was going to happen to me or to them.

Strangely, I never worried about Chad much. While he had a dangerous career as a police officer,

I never really worried about his health. He was immortal to me. He was larger than life. He could do anything. He could fix anything. *He really could fix anything.* So, even after we were told he had pancreatic cancer, I still figured he would fix it and he would never succumb to it. Nothing could beat him. Nothing could take him down. If anybody was going to beat this, it was going to be him. He was so strong. So resilient. He never complained. In fact, when he was having chemo, he never missed a day of work, he actually gained weight and that beautiful picture of him that circulates on the internet was actually taken in the middle of his treatment. In my mind, this cancer was not going to defeat him.

And then suddenly, on a mild, sunny day in June, it did.

He died. The fight was over. Cancer won. *You have no idea how much I hate cancer.*

All of the hope I had melted and puddled at my feet. I sloshed through it the best I could, but the defeat was insurmountable. He was not supposed to die. I don't care if stage 4 pancreatic cancer has a 1% five-year survival rate, he was going to be the 1%. And, sure, maybe everybody else expected it, but I didn't. Even in the hospital those few days before, it never crossed my mind that his death was impending. No, he was going to survive. I was sure of it.

So, when he didn't, it was devastating. It was heartbreaking. It was a nightmare. But, that's not what this chapter is about. This chapter is not about those emotions. I write plenty of those chapters but this one is not about that part of grief. It's about the fear.

For the first time, ever, I was truly faced with my own mortality. While I have thought about it my whole life, it was always abstract. Just kind of out there somewhere. It was a thought. But as I watched my 45-year-old husband die, it became this weird reality. In a few months, I will be 46. I will be older than him. That's not right. It's so surreal. He has always been older than me. Since I was 15, he was always been one year, eight months and 15 days

217

older than me. Yet, in two months, I will now be older than him because his life stopped, and mine didn't.

What it means is that it could have been me. It could have been you. It could have been anybody. If he could die, so could I.

I was busy the first year. I was in a fog. I didn't think that much about it. Maybe there was part of me that felt like I was "protected" from further harm because we had just faced this tragedy and it would be totally unfair for a second tragedy to hit. I ignored the articles I read about it, about how whole families were killed in awful accidents or a father died, and a mother died shortly after. I refused to listen to stories where husbands and wives died within months of each other. I absolutely decided without any doubt that while my heart was hurting, I would not allow myself to die of a broken heart.

Yet, as life goes on and the pressure and weight sit on me, as a widow and a single mom, I am tired. I am exhausted. And, I can feel it. Every day there is a new ache or pain. Every day, I am tired. Every day I am trying to figure out how to stretch the hours to be more productive. Every day I am telling myself I need to be healthier. Eat healthier. Exercise. Every day I worry if I have a cough for too long. Every day I feel like I can't take a deep breath and every day I have every reason why it's not just anxiety. Every day I panic if my head aches in a way I have never felt before. Every day that I wake up and my arm hurts from sleeping on it the wrong way, I'm pretty sure it's because I am having a stroke. He did. His arm hurt before we knew what was causing it. If he can have a stroke, couldn't I?

The answer is yes. Yes, I could.

But then I remember that it was cancer that caused his stroke, not anything else. Could I get cancer like he did? The answer is yes. Yes, I could. But, do I have cancer now? No. Not that I know about, at least.

So, I have two choices. I can live in the shadow of his cancer and in unspeakable fear, or I can live my life in the way in which it was meant to be lived. A life with purpose, love, and direction. The direction in my life has changed, just as the lives of all people who have suffered loss. It used to be mapped out perfectly as I walked alongside the man I loved, but now that he is gone, I have a new map. That map is hard. It's tiring. It's fearful at times. But, it is not undoable.

Your map is not undoable, either. And what I have found is, that many, many, many people who have experienced the death of a loved one, or who has been the caretaker of somebody during a disease identifies with this in some way. It is normal to be more scared of things. It is normal to look at things differently than you did before. It is normal to be more worried. I'm not diagnosing myself or anybody else, but I imagine there is some post-traumatic stress in play here. I know for me, I am always second guessing myself with his treatment, but also if I missed the warning signs before he was diagnosed. Yet, interestingly, every time I feel like something might be wrong with me, the last thing I want to do is get it checked out. Because there is no way I want that same kind of news. I don't know why I think avoidance is helpful, because it's really not.

So, I have made a doctor's appointment for a check-up and have been very honest with him about my fear and anxiety. Same with my OB and my GI doctor and my dentist, even. I want them to know what fears I have, and I want them to address them. I want them to make sure they're checking for the right things, I want them to make sure they're not cutting any corners and if all it is an anxiety, then I want them to be aware of that, too. I want to trust them with my story. For so long I was my husband's advocate, and now – I have to be my own.

You might wonder why I have a GI doctor. I have one because my husband died of pancreatic cancer and had no GI problems before his diagnosis. So, "my" GI doctor was actually "his" GI doctor. After my husband died, I started supporting research and awareness for pancreatic cancer. I remember being in the GI doctor's office and telling him how frustrated I was that there was no early detection, or any real treatment and I could have pancreatic cancer right now and not even know. He told me it was unlikely and listed out the reasons why. I nodded and almost gave up and then thought – "No. Here I am telling people all over the world to take charge of their own healthcare and I am not just going to take his word for it." So, after some more discussion, he said to me with a smile on his face, "You're not leaving here until I approve some tests, are you?" I shook my head and told him no and he did exactly what I needed him to do. He didn't do it because he thought I had cancer. He did it because he wanted to offer me peace of mind. And, he did.

So, as much as I worry, I also know that I have to work through that fear and have a support team in place when need be, whether that's family, friends or even medical professionals. It's important to know it's normal, but it's just as important to be proactive. You have to take care of you.

It's ok to be honest with the people you trust. As crazy as you might feel, or as weird as it might be to admit these things, so much of it is normal and so much of it is something else somebody else is also feeling. It's so important to know you're not alone, but the only way to really know that is to seek out people who understand and to open up to them.

It might be scary, it might be intimidating, it might be totally uncomfortable, but at the end of the day, it might just be exactly what you need.

It could always be worse

"To talk without thinking is to shoot without aiming." – Proverb

People have actually dubbed me an "expert" on grief. I am not sure why. It's flattering to be an "expert" at something, but at the same time, I wish it wasn't a topic I had any experience in. While I have a lot to say about grief, I think everybody who has experienced it is a true expert, just by the fact that they are living it, day in and day out. Therefore, when I am thinking about the things I want to write, I know the best wisdom comes from a collective group of people who share the same stories and feel the same loss. Sometimes, I know what I want to say and sometimes, I reach out -usually via social media- to see what other people's thoughts are and how they align with my own. This book would not be complete without a chapter on what to say and what not to say to the grieving person the following is a list of things I have compiled from basically, just asking around.

For me, I have a hard time with the phrase, "I'm sorry". I am very aware that when a loss happens, some people don't know what to say and saying, "I'm sorry" is the only thing they can think of. As a grieving person, I want you to say *something*. I want you to acknowledge what's going on. I want to know you're there for me. So, if the only words you can push out are those, then keep doing it. But, when I hear of a loss, *of course I am sorry*. It's the obvious choice. Everybody is "sorry", and after a while, it starts to feel impersonal. To be honest, when you say you're "sorry" because you don't know what else to say, we don't know what to say, either. A polite "thank you" might be all you get because we agree. We're all sorry. I try not to use the phrase very often, but I still do because even I sometimes don't know what to say when in an uncomfortable situation. So, I try to think of what I would want to hear in the face of any loss. What we

225

want you to say instead is, "I'm sorry. I am here for you." Or, "I'm sorry, I baked you a cake." Or, "I'm sorry, Let me take your kid for an hour." Or, "I'm sorry, I remember when (he/she) did _____. It made me laugh so hard." Because when you're thinking about what to say, one of the best things you can say is something you miss about them, too. We *yearn* for people to talk about them. We want to hear their name. We want to know you miss them, too. We don't want you to be afraid to talk about them. We take comfort in it. We want to hear about them so bad. We want to talk about them without it being weird. Without making *you* uncomfortable. Open the door for us.

The best response I received? "Take it easy, amigo." I don't know why I loved it so much. Maybe because it was different. Maybe because it wasn't trying to solve anything. Maybe because it was cliché. Maybe because it seemed genuine. Maybe because it was the right words that I needed to hear at the time. It was sent to me by an old high school friend who I wasn't particularly close to in high school. But for some reason, it made me *want* to talk to them when I was in the worst stage of my grief. It just struck me for some reason. I guess, because to me, what it really meant was, "this sucks and I see that." Or, "I'm not going to blow smoke up your skirt, just try to hang in there."

We want to hear you say you love us. That you care about us. That you can imagine it really sucks. But what we don't want to hear is this:

1.   **"It could always be worse."** Really? How? It can be worse in what way? Like, if my whole family was wiped out? A meteor hit the house? Yeah, I guess that would be worse. Regardless if it really "could have been worse", it's unnecessary to say that. Because, when crisis hits you, trust me, there really is *nothing* worse.

2.   **"Are you okay?"** The simple answer is, 'no', and I don't know when I will be. Please don't ask somebody that. We are not okay. We may start to be okay some days, but we are never okay full

227

time. We are trying to accept that and make peace with that. We can barely explain it to ourselves, much less to somebody else.

3.   **"When your number Is called, there's not much you can do."** My friend who lost her son submitted this and I almost gasped when I heard it, only because if she submitted it, then somebody must have said it to her. Are we playing bingo? God is calling numbers now? If that's the case, then can I win the lottery instead?

4.   **"He/She is in a better place".** Oh really? What place is that? My immediate answer is "no." Besides the fact that not all spouses left behind are people of faith, let's face it, it's a crappy thing to say to somebody who has lost their person. There is no better place for them to be than with you, in your home, in your bed and at every event in your life. Even as a Christian, nobody really takes comfort that they might be in your version of Heaven, and not with them. It doesn't ease our pain. It doesn't make us less angry, in fact, it might just get you taken off

the Christmas card list, because our entire life is full of "whys" and unanswered questions that make it close to impossible to rationalize their loss. So, when you tell us they're in a better place, you're insinuating it's a good thing, and trust me, it's not. However, I have had beautiful conversations with people about their beliefs that have brought me much needed peace. If they ask you, share them. If they don't, please don't lecture.

5.   **"Let me know what you need"**. Ok, I'm guilty of this, too, and I should get better at it. Nobody, in the face of great loss, knows what they need. Don't assign that to me. Don't make me figure out a job. We can't even figure out how to get out of bed some days, please don't make us figure out something for you to do, too. Because we never will. Personally, I was so fortunate to have friends just show up on my doorstep; some bringing food, some Kleenex, some alcohol, and some just came to sit quietly while I cried. I thank God for those people. The best text a grieving person can get is, "I'm

229

coming over at 3 to do your laundry. Send me your garage code".

6.   **"Time heals".** No, it really does not. In fact, the second-year sucks more. We walk around in a fog the first year and by the second year, reality hits. That's when you should show up. Because that's when you're really falling apart. I've heard the third year gets even worse because people forget. Everybody has to go back to their own lives, that's for certain. But please don't forget time isn't fixing it. Maybe it's become less raw, but it's still there. And there are still times when panic sets in, and grief hits again.

7.   **"You're doing it wrong".** Grieving wrong, dating too soon wrong, not dating soon enough wrong, parenting wrong, driving wrong, eating wrong, you name it, we're wrong and people will tell you. They will actually come out and tell you. I'm sorry, but please, please stop. We know right from wrong. We know what we're doing and not doing. We know what seems right and what doesn't.

But unless you've walked this journey, you don't get to sit in a place of judgment. You don't get to tell us what to do or what not to. I have some tricky friends. I've heard the phrase, "I love you, and whatever you decide, I'm in your corner". Yes, yes, yes and yes again. Maybe they don't agree with me on everything, and maybe they subtly guide me back on track, but they don't judge me. Please don't judge them. A widow/widower has done something you haven't. They've fulfilled their vows. They went to bed one night a wife and woke up the next morning not being a wife anymore. You can't fathom what that is like. So please, while we're figuring it out, just be there to support us or catch us when we fall, but don't trip us in the process.

8.   **"It's the new normal".**   Oh, how I hate this one. There's nothing normal about this, and it will probably never be normal again. I don't know what to replace this with. I don't know what you're supposed to say. But to insinuate that this is "normal" is ludicrous. It's not. It's not the plan we had in our

heads, it's not the way we envisioned things. Let us process it. But please don't ever tell us it's just the way it is now. Let us get to that place on our own. I have some grieving friends who have accepted this as the "new normal". But let us decide what is normal and what isn't. Let us label it.

9.   **"God needed another angel".** Ok, then please, let God find somebody else.

10.   **"At least he had a full life."** Or "At least he wasn't a child." Because their value to us decreases with age?

11.   **"It's God's Plan."** Please do not ever say that to a terminally ill patient or their family. If it's God's Plan, it's an awful one.

12.   **"Everything happens for a reason."** The strange thing with this one is that sometimes I actually believe this. I agree that things happen in the way they're supposed to that make other things happen; as in a natural order of things. But I cannot and probably will never find the reason why my husband is dead in the middle of our lives.

13.   **"God won't give you anything you can't handle."** Yes, He will. He did. I can't handle this. I am, because I have no choice, but He didn't hand pick me and my family or you and yours because you're strong enough. He didn't point and decide one day to choose us. Please don't put that on us. None of us want to be "strong enough" to handle the death or the loss of the people or things we love; please don't make us consider the fact that maybe we need to start acting "less strong" or weak so that nothing more happens in our lives.

14.   **"I know how you feel."** Please don't say this unless you have experienced loss and even then, maybe saying "I get it" is better than "I know how you feel", only because you don't know how I feel, just like I don't know how you feel. I'm not in your head. You're not in mine. I can empathize, but I really don't know exactly how you feel.

15.   **"I'm sure he would have wanted you to..."** I'm not even sure what he would have

wanted me to do. Unless he specifically told you what he wanted me to do, don't tell me you know.

We appreciate your support. We ache for your kindness. We want you to be in our lives. We want to know we're not alone. And while there's a lot not to say (or do), here's some of the things that help.

DO talk about our husbands/wives. Personally, I seek out people who knew my husband because I want you to tell me what you remember about him. It makes me feel less alone in my grief.

DO check in on us. It's ok to reach out.

DO talk about your own stuff. We're not going to break if you tell us your problems. In fact, most of us want to talk about something else.

DO keep asking us to go out. Or to come over. We might say "no" a hundred times, but eventually, we'll say "yes". Eventually we will be ready.

DO keep on loving us. Even when we're un-loveable.

DO say, "I care about you.", "I recognize your pain and how unfair this is.", "It hurts me to see you hurting because I love you."

We're tired. We're sad for sure. We're in a weird place. But don't give up on us. Just love us through it. Just try to understand and we will do our best to understand, too.

Falling in love again

"Brave girl, it's time to love again", The Better Man Project

Dear Chad,

I wrote you this letter yesterday. This was the beginning:

"I don't know how to write this letter. I don't know how to tell you this. I don't know what words to choose. I don't know how to explain this to have it make sense. I am nervous even to write the sentence. I have fallen in love again."

I went on to explain it - to tell you in this awkward way that I have found a new love. Not one that replaces my love for you, but one that has allowed me to love you both. One that has only asked for space in my heart and does not demand the whole thing. For he knows with certainty that while I love him deeply, *I will never not love you.*

236

I will be honest. I didn't love it. I had a friend read it. She liked it. But, I still felt like my emotions were all over the place and it just didn't feel right. It didn't settle like most of these chapters do. Even though I had my reservations about it, I was still going to publish it. It might have felt rough, but the content was what was important, and that was conveyed.

That I had fallen in love again.

I saved the document, closed my computer, then remembered I needed to make a change. I quickly opened up the laptop again, opened "word" and looked for the document. I didn't panic right away when I couldn't find it. I just kept looking. First where I saved it, then in places I know I didn't just to be sure, then searched for it by name, then looked in recent documents. It was gone. Completely erased, like it never existed.

I know many people will say it was a fluke, and I suppose it could have been. I suppose it could have just been one of those things where the document you're working on disappears. I was a little irked for sure but decided not to let it upset me too much. It was only three hours of work, not three days and I would just try again.

So, today, I prepped my computer again, ready to start over. I turned it on, brought up a blank page, picked a playlist which this time happened to be John Denver. Don't ask, I don't know why. It was the first link I clicked on. "Sunshine on My Shoulders" I think. I got distracted for a minute as the song played, and about halfway through, I started putting my thoughts together again on paper. I typed and typed, a couple of paragraphs until the music stopped and then picked up again.

Weird thing though, it wasn't John Denver this time. It was Pink Floyd's "Wish You Were Here", which as you know was the song I played for you at your funeral. Why did it come up while I was writing a chapter on new love after the original document erased itself? I know what the skeptics will say, but I also know you – and I know you are

238

always here. Maybe you don't like the topic. Maybe you think you're funny. But yes, I miss you, too.

By the way, as soon as that song was over, John Denver came right back on. And now, as I am writing this, the playlist must've "fluked" again, because Gerry Rafferty's "Right Down the Line" just started playing out of nowhere. It's not even on "sort" or "shuffle". It just keeps "messing" up. But, I know what's happening here. Because, I know, *like you do* – it was "our song" and twice now while writing this book, I've heard it, even though it's an old song and not particularly popular. Want to know how else I know it's you? Because it's not even *my* playlists that I'm listening to, and they weren't the same playlists each time it's happened.

I wonder what you're trying to tell me. Maybe you're just saying hi. Whatever it is, I am glad you still come around, even though so much has changed. I am glad you show up, even though life is so different now.

But then again, you always have.

239

Not long before you died, you found me in the kitchen trying to open something. Do you remember? I was holding it upside down and having a fight with it. You sauntered over, took it from my hand, held it right side up, opened it and handed it back to me. You looked me for a minute, then quietly asked, "Who is going to take care of you when I am gone?" I shook my head. "That will never happen. You're not going anywhere." I was emphatic about it. I believed you were never leaving. You had been loyal, consistent, honest and I never doubted your love and commitment to me, or to us. Yet, forces out of our control took you away, and left me alone. But, your question never left me. I think you knew I could reasonably take care of myself, but I also think you knew that I really didn't want to. And you also knew that somebody would have to be there to open cans and explain things to me. You knew that, and I think you knew this man before he even came to me. I really believe that. You sent signs, all the time. And it was those signs that made me feel so comfortable with my choice. I had a dream one night, and I am sure you were here. He and I were standing in the garage talking, when you pulled up in a little blue sportscar. I cautiously walked towards the car that already had the window down and peeked in. You were sitting in the driver's seat looking up at me, smiling. Oh, that sheepish grin. You told me to get in. In slow motion, I looked at him. He motioned for me to go with you. I climbed in and you caught his attention and spoke these simple words – "I will bring her right back." He nodded, and we left. I remember very little after that, but I do remember you were so happy. You were so happy. You were excited to show me everything in your car and kept repeating, "You're never going to believe this", and "You're never going to believe what they have there." I have no doubt you were showing me your Heaven. And you were also showing me how happy you are, and how it was ok for me to be happy here. Maybe it was permission, I don't know, but I am learning how to be happy again, I really am. Yet, that happiness does not come without fear. I am so scared to lose somebody again, but I am trying so hard to love again without that curse. Chad, you know how I write you letters and leave them at your grave? It's because writing is the one way I know how to communicate. It's the one way I know how to uninhibitedly express myself. It's the only way I know how to be raw and transparent. So, I wrote to him and I want to share it with you. I see widows all the time posting on the internet about how they have healed and how they're complete now, but sometimes I question that. Sometimes, I am not so sure they are being painfully honest. Sometimes, I think it is unrealistic. Sometimes, I think this is what they really need to be saying:

Dear You,

I am supposed to write you a letter like all the other women on the internet do when they find somebody after they've lost their great love. I am supposed to write you a letter thanking you for coming into my life. I'm supposed to write a letter thank you for taking care of me, and my child, and list out all of your greatness. I am supposed to write you a letter telling you how extraordinary you are. How caring you are. How my heart is full. I am supposed to tell you how amazing you are. And how you have stepped into big shoes and how you have taken on this role so brilliantly, even though it is a role I'm sure you've never thought you would have. I am supposed to gush over you and tell you and everybody else how happy I am and how you have healed my heart and how I wasn't ready to love again but you came in and whisked me off my feet and made me believe in happy endings. Yes, I am supposed to tell you how thankful I am for you. And how much I appreciate you. How indebted I am to you for loving the broken me. I need you to know that this is all true. It is all accurate and exactly how I feel. It will never be lost on me how lucky I am to have two of you in my life. Two perfect men for me. Two great loves. Two of you who captured my heart and how lucky I am to be able to walk this wondrous life with, one

243

before the other. But I have to tell you something else. I have to write this letter. Dear You, I am terrified. I am so scared. Because the last time I felt this way, he left. He didn't want to, of course. It was out of his control. But, my heart still bleeding. And I am still petrified. There are so many times when my happiness lives in a place of fear. There so many times when my heart is confused. There are so many times when I am waiting for the bad to come. There are so many times when I am waiting for you to be ripped away from me. And, it will never be the big things that trigger that. No. It will be Sunday mornings over coffee, or Tuesday nights talking about the day. It will come watching you sleep, or singing in the car, or high fiving you when something finally went right. It will come when you make me laugh, when you hold me tight, and when you rejoice in some success. Because those are the moments when I memorize you. Those are the moments when I breathe you in and try to hold my breath. Those are the moments that are so raw, and so real, that I

244

cannot help but fear losing them. That fear turns to dread. It becomes anxiety. I am suddenly terrorized with the idea of losing you and feeling that pain all over again. So, I push. In spite of how meant for me you are, I will push you away. I will sabotage and pick fights and cut you off at the knees. I will attack, and I will insult, and I will try to get you to leave. In fact, maybe sometimes, I will actually tell you to go. Because I am so afraid to feel that loss again. I am afraid to feel like everything is out of my control again. I am afraid to be helpless again. I am afraid to live in limbo again and not know what the end result will be. I am sorry. I am truly sorry. I have lost before, but loss is not exclusive to me. Many people have lost before, and so many have learned to love again. To heal. To move forward. I want that so bad, and I am working on achieving that every day. I know I have no right to ask, but please, please be patient with me. I am healing my mind. I am healing the way I think. I am healing from the shock and total despair. But you, you are healing my heart. And it might take time for me to trust that. It might take time for me to believe that something good can happen. It might take time to feel like you're not leaving, too. So, thank you you for taking care of me, and my child, and for being full of greatness. Thank you for being extraordinary. Thank you for being amazing. You have stepped into big shoes. You have taken on this role so brilliantly even though I know it is not a role you ever thought you would have. You are showing me how to be happy again. I wasn't ready to love again but you came in and whisked me off my feet and are making me believe in happy endings. Yes, I am thankful I am for you. I appreciate you. I am indebted to you for loving the broken me. My heart...is full.

Love, Me

Chad, I do not know how to move on completely. Like so many people, I am just putting one foot in front of the other trying to make it work.

Trying to feel again. Trying to love again. Strangely, it never felt like I was cheating on you. We took vows, and we honored those vows. We said it, out loud, "Until death do we part". We did that. We made it. We made it through a whole lifetime. And, now, it is time for me to live a lifetime with somebody else. It's a strange and freakish thought sometimes. We didn't choose to leave each other. We didn't have a nasty divorce. We didn't split up property or argue over child support. I didn't sell my ring. Do you remember my ring? I never took it off. Ever. I had worn it for so long that to this day, you can still see the waves in my skin from where it sat on my finger. Do you remember when it came off? I know you do. Not only were things getting serious between him and me, but I had been thinking a lot about taking it off because I was afraid if something happened to it, or the diamond fell out that I would be regretful forever because you are not here to replace it. But, it wouldn't come off. It was stuck. So stuck that I thought I was going to have to cut it off to save it.

247

But one morning, when he left for work, I stood at the sink doing dishes like I had so many countless times before and as I picked up a bowl, my beautiful ring effortlessly slipped off my finger and into the bowl. I gasped and tried to put it back on, and it wouldn't go back on. No matter how hard I tried, it would not go back on. I know that was you quietly telling me to let go. I know that was you peacefully telling me to move on. I know that was you exquisitely telling me to love again. And, I am. I am loving again.

I have learned from losing you just how important it is to not waste time, and to love again with all the passion that is burned into my heart. I think you would like him. In fact, I know you would. You would be friends. You have the same interests. Same ideas. Same mannerisms even, at times. He's smart. He's funny. He loves your daughter. He plays with the dogs. He can cook. He is kind. He is generous and has a good heart. He watches stupid television shows with me. He wants to know your story. He is not intimidated by our relationship. He is not in competition. He champions your cause. He supports me unequivocally. He laughs at my jokes. He listens intently to my memories. He allows me that freedom to talk about you, and he finds joy in it. He never quiets my feelings. He never discounts them. He never makes me feel uneasy in my grief. He wipes my tears and holds my hand and makes me feel like I am home again. He loves me. He loves me in the same way you did; and the way you would have wanted me to be loved. I am so lucky to have walked the first half of my life with you and will be so lucky to walk the second half with him as he holds my broken heart close, takes my hand in his and leads me, and checks on me in the kitchen and opens my cans.

You have shown me what great love is. You have shown me what an amazing relationship feels like. I will honor that as I move forward, forever. Please, though, even as my heart heals, please – just don't go far.

Love, Me

I want my life back

"You gave me a forever within the numbered days",
John Green, The Fault in our Stars

I have skimmed over this topic in this book but haven't really dived into it. Just yesterday, I was talking to a friend about it who said to me, "It's true, it's real, and it's raw. Exactly how you feel. You've poured your heart into this. I can't imagine talking about grief and not making this statement."

I want my life back.

Maybe that sounds selfish, but I want my life back. I want my life back so bad that sometimes I can actually feel my stomach tearing from the searing pain of not having it. I want my husband back. I want my life to be the way my life was before. I want my kids to feel whole again. I want it back. All of it. I want to grab somebody, anybody, and beg them to just go get it and bring it to me. I feel this incredible amount of desperation at times where I just don't know how to do this, like this, without him.

I have said before that the minute Chad was diagnosed, everything changed. *Everything.* Our family, our relationship, how we did things, how we thought about things, the holidays, the everyday stuff with the kids, their school, our work, how we slept at night, how we spent our days, how we talked to each other, our relationships with other people, what kind of groceries we bought, how we planned things – everything. The entire atmosphere changed.

I am, by nature, a worrier and very vocal about it. I don't know if my husband worried but, if he did, he didn't talk much about it. He was the most grounded, loyal, steadfast, patient, kind man I have ever met. He was solid. He never let me, or my kids, feel like they were battling anything alone. He was never leaving me. He was never going to cheat on me. He made the decision to love me during all the good and all the bad and he meant it. I am not naïve. I am not blind. I know women say that all the time,

252

but in this case, it was the absolute truth. He was never going to hurt our marriage or leave me alone. He loved me, but he also felt responsible for me in some way. He believed that when people got married, they took care of each other. He believed that husbands and wives had a bond that should not be broken. He believed in doing the right thing, being faithful and honoring his vows. Coming from a long line of failed relationships, he restored my faith that somebody would be good to me. That they would take care of me, and I would take care of them. He didn't just make me believe in love again, he made me believe in goodness again.

At the time, after his diagnosis, I thought his love for me and my love for him did not change. Looking back, I can see now that it did. It became more intense. We were more connected. We were exposed to fear – together. For the first time in our relationship, we were scared at the same time. We had to rely on each other in a way we hadn't before. We had to hold tightly to the things that mattered.

253

We had to work through our panic. I thought we were close before his diagnosis, but it wasn't until the diagnosis and the subsequent grieving of our life that we realized how close we really were. It wasn't until the first time I saw him lying in a hospital bed hooked to devices that I knew how much, how *tortuously* much, that I loved him.

Maybe it wasn't a feeling I knew how to feel before tragedy struck, I don't know. But this man, when I saw *this man,* who never got sick and who could fix anything, lying in a bed helpless, hurting and confused, I knew my role had changed. He would still take care of me for sure, but now I would really have to step up and find ways to take care of him. It wasn't always easy. He was stubborn sometimes. I got irritated sometimes. He was frustrated. I was frustrated.

I wanted to be packing for a camping trip, not packing his surgical wound.

Does that make me selfish? I guess. I know he wanted that, too, and he was never selfish so maybe it's normal?

It wasn't that I wasn't going to do whatever he needed me to do. But, in the middle of it, I still wanted my life back. Please, somebody, just give me my life back.

Take me back to the time when everything was right. Take me back to the time when my kids were little, and life was busy and so wonderfully chaotic. Take me back to when we had a beer on the patio after a long day. Take me back to the times we had friends over and played pool and rocked out to "Don't Stop Believin" in the garage. Take me back to the time he sang into a broom, pretending it was a microphone. Take me back to the long summer days and fresh cut grass. Take me back to midnight barbeques, popcorn at the movies and Sunday morning coffee. Just take me back. Take us all back.

Because whether you realize it or not, after some kind of crisis or some kind of loss, you live in a life of grief. You live with grief sitting in your lap trying so hard to keep it away. You live in a constant state of mourning because, while you or your loved one might still be alive, the life you once had is irrevocably changed. It just is. And then you start feeling guilty about grieving when you're still living. Can the two even coexist? Shouldn't you just be thankful you're alive? If you're mourning a divorce, shouldn't you be thankful you can still love again? If you're mourning the loss of a job, shouldn't you be thankful that you still have the ability to work?

I guess the answer is "yes", but it still doesn't mean that you're not grieving. It still doesn't mean you're not in pain. It still doesn't mean you aren't struggling. It still doesn't mean you don't want your life back.

I think it's ok to want your life back. I really do. I'm not unhappy. But, I have also worked very hard at allowing my grief into my life, walking alongside me, and taking its proper place without consuming my life. Because it does have a place. It does. It is allowed in. But it is not allowed to defeat me, and it is not allowed to defeat you. It should be taken out when it needs to be taken out and put away when it needs to be put away. But, it is ok to recognize it, feel it, deal with it and move on, then repeat that process whenever you need to, whether or not your loss is permanent or not. It is ok to go through that cycle even if a death hasn't occurred.

Because death isn't the only thing reserved for grief. Sometimes, it's just the life you once had.

I also think I suffer from survivor's guilt. Admittingly, I don't know much about this. But, I do know that I feel guilty that I am still here, and he isn't. I feel badly when I have fun in my life knowing he is gone. I hate that I get to do stuff with our daughter and he doesn't. I struggle on Christmas not hanging his stocking. It's hard to enjoy steak knowing it was his favorite food.

But, I have had to find my way around that. I have had to allow myself to feel bad and feel sad about it, because it's really a sad thing. Then, I have to allow myself to come back around and enjoy this life, no matter how much I want my old life back.

I have to for me. I have to for my kids. I have to for him.

So, I will mourn the life I am missing, and I will do my best to always claw to the top of this one. I don't have to forget him or not love him or ignore the life we had to feel good about where I am now.

In fact, I think he would be pleased. And that makes my heart happy. Because him being happy for me is the biggest reminder of that life I miss so much, and the biggest source of proof that he will always be part of every life to come.

I'm hanging onto that. I am going to live. I am going to flourish. I am going to be ok.

And, so are you.

I do not want to get over my grief

"Embrace your grief. For there, your soul will grow." -Carl Jung

I don't want to "get over" my grief. No, no I do not. I have never had anybody tell me to "get over it," but I have had people say that I will get over it and that, eventually, somewhere down the line I will be done with it. First of all, I don't agree that I will ever be done with it. I don't think any of us will ever be done with it. And I don't think we will ever really get over it, nor do I want to.

I want to embrace it. Sounds odd, but I do. I want to embrace my grief and learn from it. I want to enjoy and apply all of the gifts I have been given from it. Using "grief" and "gift" in the same sentence might sound like an oxymoron, but it is true that grief gives the grieving person certain gifts that non-grieving people don't know about. And, for that, in some sense, we're lucky.

I have said and written often about how, during a cancer diagnosis, people start their grief process at that moment. It's not dissimilar from the grief process we know about in the "Five Stages of Grief," but not only do you start to grieve the person who is still alive, but you grieve your life as you once knew it. While normal and predictable, it's also very confusing. It's weird to grieve somebody you love when you can still look at them, talk to them and hold them. And when they do pass, your grieving is still there, along with all sorts of other emotions you're trying to process, and your grief process is not so clean. It's not a 1-2-3-4-5 process that starts and finishes. You don't really know what "stage" you're in, because you're not starting from the beginning and you're not really at the end. You're in some middle, puzzling state of existence.

Therefore, my first "grief gifts" came when Chad was still living. After his diagnosis, everything changed. I remember one of the first, very clear grief gifts I received was no longer caring what people thought about me, him, or our life. No matter our personality, we all care on some level. It's human nature. But, I went through a period of time where I *really* did not care. I remember somebody telling me something they thought about me one night and I heard the first part of what they were saying until, eventually, all I heard was "wah, wah, wah," like Charlie Brown's teacher in the old cartoons. What they were saying to me in that moment was so unimportant and so insignificant that while it might have bothered me before that, it didn't that time. Not only did it not bother me, but it was at that moment where I knew, without a doubt, how free I was from the outside world. I knew what my priority was at that instant. One single priority had never been so clear to me up until then. And, it wasn't the person in front of me.

I also realized during that time who I wanted in my life and who I didn't. I didn't realize this until right before he died, but I was subconsciously taking mental notes of how people treated me or him or my kids and was making decisions about who I would allow into my life and who I wouldn't. So, when he died, I as so angry about his death and so frustrated with some people that I actually envisioned myself at his funeral turning them away if they showed up. Thankfully, they did not, but I was ready. I don't know why it was so important to me at the time, but I was ready to do it. By God, I was going to make my point. I was going to show them that they could not be awful to us one day and put on fake grief the next. They didn't get to have that. They didn't get to experience that with me. They didn't get to be part of that process.

After he died, it quickly became apparent who was there for us and who was not. This brought the loss of people I thought were my friends, and the gain of real friends who were previously strangers. It's true - some of your best friends become strangers and strangers become your best friends. It was another grief gift to have such clarity because, at the time, none of us needed the drama. And, while there were experiences that were very hard, I did learn that it's ok to let go sometimes. It's ok to let people leave your life. It's ok to change your surroundings because that might be the exact thing you need. It's ok to move forward, even if some people don't go with you.

I have also learned that it's ok to feel what true grief is. It's ok to not be ok. I have said that so many times before, but it's one of the truest statements there is. I should clarify that if you're really "not ok" that it might be time to see somebody about it. It's ok to have moments of grief, but it is not ok to never work through it.

What I mean by it is that it's very normal to feel what you do. I had a good friend experience loss recently. And what she told me was that it's like "walking through heavy snow". If you have never experienced a snow storm before, it's like walking in mud, which was another analogy she used. I equated it to quicksand, where you literally have to pick up one leg, put it down in front of you, pick up the other leg, put that down and repeat all the while feeling like you're being sucked down. It's hard. It's really hard. You're in a fog and just when you think it lifts, it comes back and the cycle repeats. But, the fact that you're doing it, no matter how hard it is, is what matters in the end. If you were really being sucked in by quicksand, you wouldn't just stand there, right? You would try to get out. You would do something. *So, keep doing it.*

We fight to get out of it, and we instinctively fight to get out of our grief. We want to claw and climb and scream and yell until we feel better. We're angry and irritable and sad and confused and lonely and frustrated all at the same time. We want people around and then we don't. We want to hang on and we want to let go. We want to cry, and we want to laugh. Nothing makes any sense. I'm not totally convinced anything will ever make sense again.

I am ok with that.

I am ok with that. I keep telling myself and you should, too. I am ok with that. I am ok with the fact that nothing will ever make sense again. I will not stand in regret. I will not get trapped in the quicksand. I will not sit in my grief. I will not be defeated by this grief. I will not be destroyed.

But, I will learn from it. I will embrace it. I will be a better version of myself because of it.

I will be more empathetic towards people's suffering because I learned that not everybody will be. I will offer my story, no matter how hard it is to repeat if it will help others because I have learned that there is strength in people coming together. I will love so much deeper than I did before because I have learned what it is like to lose love wishing you had loved more. I will be more kind because I have learned how somebody's unkind words and actions can unravel you at your weakest. I will be more appreciative of people and things, because I have learned the value in that. I will be more selective about my inner circle, because I have learned that not everybody has your best interest at heart. I will be quicker to forgive because I have learned that sometimes, you run out of time. I will be more available to receive love because I have learned that sometimes, that is all somebody has to give. I will pause more and reflect because I have learned the great lesson in re-evaluating. I will be more accepting, because I have learned how important being accepted is. I will be less judgmental, because I have learned that nobody really knows what you feel but you. I will extend my support more, because I have learned what it is like to not feel supported. I will be present in the small moments more, because I have learned how easily those can be taken away. I will take more pictures, because I have learned that the mental snapshots fade. I will be more patient because I have learned what it's like to be met with impatience. I will be less anxious, because I have learned that worrying does me no good. I will take more chances because I have learned that life is short, and those chances sometimes disappear.

No, I do not want to "get over my grief." I want to embrace it. I want to remember it. I want to learn from it. I want to allow it to make me a better person. I will never let my grief control me, but I will allow it to walk alongside of me and guide me as my life goes on. Because, it does friends. Life does go on. But, it does not have to go on sadly or with regret. Life is weird after you lose somebody you love. But, it can be – and it will be - beautiful and magical and full of wonder. *You just have to let it.*

YOU are phenomenal

"You can't be brave if you've only had wonderful things happen to you." – Mary Tyler Moore

I've said it a million times. Grief is tricky. Just as you think you're getting a handle on it, something triggers it, and the process starts again. There are things wrapped up with loss that we don't consider when it happens. At the time, we're just mourning. Sad. Torturing ourselves with "what-if's." Trying to figure out what happened. Retracing every step and then trying to figure out the future at the same time. Whether loss is expected or not, it's the same thing. It's the same feeling of sadness, hopelessness and overwhelming fear. Fear of your own mortality, your own stability and what life will be like now living with this great loss. It could be the death of a loved one. It could be divorce. Or the loss of a job. It could be any of it, or all of it. It doesn't matter. Loss is hard, and it is very, very real.

So, we start this process of healing. From day one, we cycle through it. We have good days. Bad days. Then all bad days. Then mostly good days. Then back to good and bad days. Until one day, we start feeling better and we're ready to go back out there. We're ready to take on a new love, a new job, new responsibilities, and we slowly and, sometimes, subconsciously add those things back into our lives. Then, just as suddenly, a trigger comes up that reminds us of what loss feels like, and we panic. We get scared. And we start waiting for the other shoe to drop.

Since Chad's death, I have experienced more loss. I don't need to get into the details to make you understand, but it's tough. Loss is one thing, but loss compounded is overwhelming. After my husband died, I sat in that for a while. I sat in that pain. Without even knowing it, I went back to real life over the course of two years and started allowing all the pressures and stress back in. There was a time where I didn't care about anything but my healing and that

269

of my children, and during that time, I didn't care what anybody thought, or what anybody did. It was liberating. But, as time went on, reality came back with a vengeance. My priorities changed again, I started putting myself back out there and I started to live again.

But the problem was, I never lived without the fear. I was always waiting for something to happen. I was always waiting for the bad to come. I was always surrounded by doubt and anxiety. I was constantly worried. When my husband had cancer, we were obviously in and out of the doctor's office all the time. And each time, I sat in the lobby and asked myself, "Is today the day they tell us the cancer is back?" "Is today the day they tell us there is nothing more they can do?" "Is today the day he dies?"

That feeling has never gone away. I now live my life with that cloud surrounding me. That burden of tragedy. That curse of my past. I often question how I will ever get past that; how I will ever be "normal" again, or if there is even such a thing.

During my subsequent losses, I have blamed myself. I have told myself that if I had just "done this", or just "did that", that this would not be happening. If I hadn't been so worried, it would not have happened. If I didn't have this fear hanging over me, it would have been ok.

And then, today, it dawned on me. *This was not a self-fulfilling prophecy*. This was not all my fault, and I refuse to take blame for one more second. Because, while all of my loss has been hard and has affected me in negative ways, it has also taught me amazing lessons, and I have to start remembering that. I have to start realizing that it's ok to live. It's ok to be happy. It's ok to enjoy moments and not worry they will be taken away. But it's also shown me this:

1. **I am a strong person, even when I feel like I am not.** Because when you bury a spouse,

or a child, or a parent, or your best friend, you do something that not everybody can do. That puts you in a club nobody wants to be part of, but at the same time, it means you're a badass. You're the elite. You are the Navy Seal in a world full of sailors. YOU are indestructible because you loved somebody so much that you could hold their hand while they died and stand by their gravesite to wish them farewell. YOU are amazing because you lost your job, yet you got up the next day to look for another one. YOU are fierce because you lost a great love and put yourself back out there to try again. YOU are resilient. YOU are a commanding force, and don't you ever forget that.

2.　　**This is not the end of your story.**
No, no it is not. It is just the beginning. It is a painful chapter in your life, and it is awful to live through it. While painful, it will shape you. And you get to decide how. I chose to be fearful. Maybe you have, too. But I choose not to be anymore. I choose to write my story with permanent ink and be proud of who I

am, and where I've come from, even if I fail sometimes. Because, it's ok. It's ok to trip up and fall, but it is not ok to stay there.

3.   **I can do this. In fact, I can do anything.** And, so can you. I watched my husband take his last breath and I fulfilled my vows to him. How many people today can say that? I did it. You did it. We took it seriously. For better, for worse, in sickness and in health, until death do we part. You took a child from your womb and loved him and cared for him and poured life into him and then stood with grace while his soul left his body, never once leaving his side. Nobody can survive that without being so intensely and profoundly phenomenal. WE did it. We should be proud of ourselves. We should be shouting it from the rooftops and telling anybody who will listen. We did it. And, we survived. No, we flourished. We excelled. We took life on and looked death in the face and came out the other side.

I'm trying to remember these things today, and I will probably need to remind myself of it over and over. Because even I get mixed up in the emotions and fear and everything that goes along with it. But, I refuse to let it define me in a negative way. I refuse to let it defeat me. I refuse to give up, and I refuse to give in. I refuse to let it dictate the rest of my life. There will be people who come and go, jobs that come and go, difficult situations, trying times, but the right people will be there, and they will never leave, no matter what. And, in that face of adversity, we will see people like us who have dug their feet in and decided to love us through it. And we will keep healing. In five years, ten years, twenty years, we will keep doing it. Because we're the real deal. We're the real bruised and bloody package and that makes us worthy. That makes us invaluable. That makes us the best of the best. Don't you ever forget who you are. Don't you ever forget your worth, and don't you ever forget how far you've come. And, I won't either.

A new friend of mine told me something today, I want to share it with you. It has been his motto for years, and now it is mine. Let it be yours.

"And, in the face of adversity, I shall stand defiant."

Think about that. Absorb that. Live that. Stand in defiance of your fears. Stand in defiance of your heartbreak. Stand in defiance of obstacles. Stand in defiance of your pain. Stand in defiance of your circumstances. Stand in defiance of your past. Just stand.

Goodbyes are harder now

"Could we see when and where we are to meet again, we would be more tender when we bid our friends goodbye". Ouida

Goodbyes are harder now. I don't even think I realized that until this weekend.

When my son left for the military three years ago, he was seventeen and I was excited for him. I was excited for him to go start his life and proud of him for choosing to serve his country. At the time, Chad had been diagnosed but when my son left, there were no signs of any tumors on Chad's imaging tests, and the naïve me thought we were in the clear. We were living out life like the storm had passed, and we were going to make it through unscathed. So, off he went to bootcamp, and my heart was happy.

The next time I would see him would be when Chad died. And the time after that, six months later, at Christmas. During both of those visits, I was still in a fog. An ugly, deep, gray fog that was hard to breathe through. I couldn't concentrate on much of anything, and even after he left, nothing seemed real. I was in a half existence, just going through the motions dizzy from holding my breath most of the time.

It's been over two years now since Chad passed away. *God, that's still so hard to type out.* It's still so hard to believe. I still expect him to walk through the door sometimes. I still hold secrets and stories because I think he's going to come home one day for me to tell him. I know he's not coming back, but my subconscious still won't let me believe it all the time. It's a surreal state of living.

This past weekend, I was lucky. After one year, seven months and four days, I got to surprise my son when he was sent someplace close, at least close enough for me to jump on a plane and show up. I'm afraid to fly, you know. But, when Chad was sick, I didn't have a choice and I jumped on as many planes as he did for treatment, as much as I could. I did it without thinking and without fear, because I just knew it was something I had to do. And this past weekend was no different. I had to see my son.

He was surprised. We got to spend some time together. On top of it, I got to see my step-son, his sweet family and my daughter and my mom as well. All was right in the world for fourteen hours.

And, then it happened. He had to leave. I thought I would just walk him to his car, hug him and say goodbye, content with the visit and the idea that it won't be long until I get to see him full-time again. But that didn't happen. It was my turn to be surprised. This time, by how I felt.

It all came rushing back. Panic. Fear. Tears. A lump in my throat. Heaviness in my chest. Fire on my skin. *Why did he have to go? When was I going to see him again? Why was I feeling this way?* He's just going back to "work", and he will be back. I reminded myself of that over and over. But, it did not keep me from wanting to

278

grab ahold of him and pull him back and beg him not to go. I didn't cry while he was leaving. I waited until he drove away, made my way into the bathroom, and sobbed. My stomach hurt. I just wanted him to come back.

I realized at that moment that I really miss my kids. I miss them as they're all living their lives, and I always have. But, I am so much more in tune with missing them now because I now know what loss feels like, and I don't want to experience it again. I realized that I am not the same as I was before. I have said before that there is this break in my life; before Chad died and after Chad died. And the "after Chad died" me is still hurting, and I assume always will.

And, every now and then that hurt is going to seep out in ways I am not prepared for, and in ways I least expect. I am trying to get used to that. To prepare for that as much as possible. To expect it. To not be blindsided. To not be scared.

And to not let my fear get in the way of living.

279

Because not living, not flourishing, and being scared for the rest of my life would be the biggest injustice to Chad that I could possibly do. My children not living their lives independent of me would be sad and awful and something that Chad would have never wanted for them.

He would have wanted us to keep living. He would have wanted us to keep exploring. He would have wanted us to keep going. *Just keep going.* He would have wanted us to love, be loved, be adventurous, and achieve our goals. And he would have wanted us to do that in the absence of fear and regret.

That's what I intend to do. No matter how hard "goodbye" is now, or how hard it is to let go, or how hard it is to believe that this will not be the last time I will see them, or how hard it is not to be afraid of tragedy, we will keep going. We will keep loving. We will keep being loved. We will keep flourishing and we will keep being finding the beauty in the world.

We will not be victims of his cancer. *No, one was enough.*

If I can offer you one last piece of unsolicited advice; do not let your loss defeat you. Do not give into fear. Do not give up. Say "hello" with a smile and warm hug and say "goodbye" with a longer hug and a heart full of peace.

Goodbye, my love

"How lucky I am to have something that makes saying goodbye so hard." – Winnie the Pooh

Chad was solitary most of the time. He liked it that way. He kept his circle tight and didn't allow many people close. I don't know why, he never said. It wasn't because he didn't like people; after all, he spent the last part of his life serving them.

He didn't require close interaction. It wasn't a necessity. He was kind, and he was generous, but it wasn't often he handed out hugs just to hand them out. If he did, it meant something. It's what made him so genuine.

When he was admitted into the hospital, whether it was for surgery or near the end, I wanted to stay with him. Just like any other wife would, I wanted to be there in the middle of the night if he needed me. Sometimes he wanted me there, sometimes he didn't, but I knew that was my place.

They always had a couch or a chair I could sleep in, and I didn't hesitate to move it close to his bed, instructing them to move the IV to the other side because I wanted to be close enough to reach out to him in the middle of the night if he needed me to.

One night, he did. He woke up in silence and called my name. He asked me to lay with him. I made my way through all the IV's and monitors and found a place next to my husband in the hospital bed. For a brief second, I wondered what the nurses would say if they found me there, then quickly decided I just didn't care. It was unlike him to call upon me for anything and I was taking full advantage of it.

I stayed there with him, just lying there, wide awake listening to him breathe. I counted his breaths. I tapped my finger to his heartbeat. I tried not to move. I didn't want to bother him.

Eventually, I had to go back to my own makeshift bed, and we never said another word about it. In fact, after that night, he barely spoke at all. I talked to him, though. I told him it was ok to go, I

283

told him I would take care of Kaitlyn, and I told him we would be alright. It wasn't ok for him to go, really, but what else was I supposed to say, except give him permission. He asked me often who would take care of me after he was gone. I think sometimes he worried about that and hung on as long as he could.

I don't know why he asked me to lay down with him that night. Maybe it was his way of saying "goodbye". Maybe that man with the rough exterior who showed love by "doing", instead of "saying", was quietly whispering his farewell, just by holding onto me one last time.

This is my reality. This is real life. These are the heartbreaking thoughts of a widow. It's been so hard, but I learned something from it. If you've lost somebody you love, I hope you can look back and remember that moment, that one single, solitary moment when they showed you how much they loved you, and I hope you cling to it fiercely, and forever. I hope that you never let that feeling go, because as you move on in life, you're going to need it. Whether you move, take a new job, meet somebody new, love again-whatever the case may be, you will feel change. And sometimes, change will be great, and sometimes, it won't be. And in those times when it's not, you have to remember that at one point, somebody loved you so much, recognized your value so much, adored you so much that while faced with their own struggle, they showed you anyway. They would want you to know that you are magnificent, and you should never forget that.

And if you still have the one you love, cherish it. Maybe they express love differently than you. Maybe they do all sorts of things that irritate you or frustrate you or make you want to run. I don't know how to fix it all, but what I do know is that when you truly love somebody, don't let the annoyances get in the way. Love them anyway. Don't let fights break you. Love them anyway. Don't let snoring get on your nerves. Love them anyway. Make them dinner. Take a minute to listen to their story. Be present. Be honest. Be willing. Be their person.

Ask them to lay with you.

You won't regret it.

Thank you for reading this. Thank you for joining me in this journey. It is my most fervent wish that you have found some clarity, some peace and that you know you're not alone.

I could not end this without sharing his eulogy. The eulogy I gave at his funeral. If you have connected with him and our story, I think you will enjoy it. *It is the last letter.*

I have included it here, so you can say goodbye to him, too because all have to say goodbye in some way. We all need some kind of closure, if that exists. Thank you for sharing in my love for him and honoring him by finding your way in your grief. Boy, do I miss him.

"Interestingly, my husband was extremely private. When he passed, I immediately called the police department to bring me the dreaded packet that was on file so that I would know what his last wishes were. Not surprisingly, he didn't fill anything

out, but when the Captain told me that the only thing he actually did fill out was that he requested a law enforcement funeral, I really had to take a step back and wrap my brain around that because he was never one to want to be the center of attention. In fact, he rarely, if ever, allowed his picture to be taken, and over the past week I've often wondered what he would have thought about the publicity surrounding his death.

I guess now we know you had a wild side, Chad. For all your years of solitude, you certainly threw us for a loop, but I guess we always knew you would have the last laugh. I knew I wanted to speak to all of you today to thank you, but in the end, I want to speak directly to Chad. Many of you have had the opportunity to watch our banter in action, but for those of you who haven't, here is a peek into our life, our laughter and the man he was.

Dear Chad,

I met you on a Tuesday. I was fifteen, you were

seventeen. I had been sick and was sitting on the back of a motorcycle about to get a ride home from a mutual friend when you and your friend pulled up in your friend's sirocco. You didn't say much as your friend and my friend talked but I remember giving you the once over, you with your flawless 80's hair, hard rock sweatshirt and perfectly pegged jeans. I tried my best to catch your eye, but all you did was muster a smile and I figured our time knowing each other had come and gone. Boy, was I wrong. And thankfully so.

You picked me up from school for our first date in your own red Sirocco with the music blaring. I quickly realized I would have to shimmy into the front seat and try to get comfortable around the massive amount of speakers in your back seat. You were the quintessential boy next store mixed with a little bit of bad boy and my heart fluttered every time I saw you. Our first date consisted of ice cream, our second was much more mature – an actual dinner at

Sizzler after your dad gave you twenty dollars and told you to take me someplace nice.

We spent many, many hot summer nights cruising around Pasadena with the likes of "Sir Mix A lot", "Ice-t", and "Bestie Boys" thumping through your speakers and had our fair share of adventures.

But the best adventures were yet to come. After losing touch for thirteen years, I remember when I received an email from you on Classmates asking if I remembered you. Remembered you? Of course, I remembered you. I had loved you from afar almost my whole life and when you weren't with me, I was always wishing you had been. When I picked myself up off the floor, I managed to email you back and was floored when you told me that you wanted to see me. Your exact words were that your sister had told you not to get married until you were 30, and you had turned 30 and couldn't think of anybody else you wanted to marry.

It was instantaneous for me and I think it was for you, too. We immediately stated making our future plans, and I'm so glad you decided to marry me even after my kids locked you out of the house for not doing what they wanted. And even more so when my aunt walked by and saw you panicking and laughed.

I am honestly struggling writing this because there is so much I want to say to you and I am finding the words escape me. I know that would shock you, but it's true. The amount of love I have for you is so difficult to express. So, for now, I will just tell you the top reasons why I am glad you are my husband.

1. Your love for ice cream never stopped. Whether it was making sundaes at home or getting ice cream with Myron on patrol, rocky road ice cream continued to be your favorite, and it was mine, too.

2. You made cupcakes with Kaitlyn. And you didn't just make cupcakes, you outfitted the kitchen with a bakery that would rival any real bakery around.

3. You could do just about anything. While anything electronic was your forte, you could seriously do anything. I've never seen anybody with so much talent, and what you didn't know, you just watched a YouTube video and suddenly you were a pro. Your talent with photography showed in your pictures at the gym, and to think you had barely owned a camera for a few months when you were already capturing the amazing action shots of your daughter and her friends.

4. Everybody loved you. Dawn and I often commented on how when you walked in the room, everything stopped. Even to the point where Linda stole our food because you needed to be fed.

5. You were hilarious. I never knew what was going to come out of your mouth, and sometimes I had to stop and ask you if you knew you had just said something out loud. Your mischievous grin led me to believe you did, but you could tell a story four times four different ways and have us laughing so hard my stomach would hurt for days.

6. Nobody left your presence without laughing, and Tabby will tell you that you even almost put her into labor once. I'm pretty sure Courtnie and I about peed our pants. I can never retell the story you told us that night the way you did, but I still giggle every time I think about it. I had no idea that on the day I gave birth to Kaitlyn that the nurse had to track you down in the hospital and told you to put scrubs on, so you could go into the operating room. I, too, would have never thought that they were just paper scrubs and that you were supposed to wear your clothes under them. So, there you were, completely naked under the paper scrubs realizing you were supposed to leave your clothes on trying to figure out how to keep them from ripping every time you moved while the doctors were operating on me. I remember you saying something about chaffing and wondering if anybody noticed.

7. You were gracious. I was so glad you were able to allow Shane to live in the house after he fell through the ceiling, but then again, he did find one of your missing tools in the attic before he came crashing down, so I guess that made it ok.

8. You played games with us, even when you didn't want to. And by the way, It's "ca-nas-ta", not "can-us-ta"

9. You were creative. One Christmas you were asked to bring an exchange gift to a party and it had to be something you didn't want. So, you took the mortgage. It was ingenious to be honest. When you stopped carrying a taser, it didn't defer you from still yelling "taser taser taser" when somebody ran from you – and it worked, the guy stopped and laid on the ground and you didn't even have to run. But my favorite was when I forgot to leave the car seat for Kaitlyn, but that was ok, you just bungee corded her to the seat.

10. You had a love hate relationship with bungee cords. I think you loved them before that infamous camping trip. I am sorry we had to take so much stuff and packed it on top of your truck so high that one of the bungee cords came flying off and

293

caught you near the eye. But the black eye suited you and gave you great stories later about having to fend off bears. On a positive note, you made a really cool truck gate and we never had to use bungee cords again. And while I'm apologizing, I am sorry I manipulated you into thinking I didn't know how to mow or paint or vacuum or iron. But you were just so much better at all of it.

11. Thank you for swinging by the house while on patrol when Savanna had her first date and staring at him. I think I actually saw his teeth chatter from fear.

12. You were generous. I often remember wondering what you were doing with our stuff when you left the house with it, but I've come to find out that you were giving it to people who needed it more than we did.

13. You were a phenomenal cook. I will miss those 1 o'clock in the morning steaks, and the side dishes you came up with on your own.

Thank you for being the best dad I have known. You not only had your own children, but you took in mine and I don't know many people at 30 who say, "let's be an instant family". But you did, and it was a lot of work, but you did it. You loved Savanna and Shane like they were your own and treated them no differently. And they loved you back. Without you, I am not sure I could have raised Savanna and Shane the way they were.

I know if you were here, you would tell Stephen how proud of him you are. Not just for his service in the Navy, but for the husband and father he himself has become. You have told me often how much you respect who he is, and how much you want him to be happy.

Kaitlyn had your heart in ways we will never fully understand. She was the only girl in your life who could get you to do anything, and let's call a spade a spade, she had you wrapped around her finger. You may never have wanted to admit that, but

I know for certain that you would have gone to the ends of the earth for her, and she knows it, too.

I cannot adequately explain how much I love you. It wasn't just about trust or respect or appreciation. I still had butterflies when I heard you come home. I wanted the world to know how incredible you were, all the time. I wanted to sing your praises to anybody who would listen because I was so enamored by you. Somebody told me once that you were a great "straight-man" for me, because we fed off of each other in ways that I am not sure everybody does. I cannot believe I don't have you here right now to tell me to stop talking.

I know this has been long winded, and I appreciate everybody hearing me out because it's important to me that Chad be honored for the person he was. I will wrap it up by telling you this, if you were his friend, you were really his friend. He did not seek attention, he did not have an overwhelming need to have people around him, he did not allow people into his life who didn't mean something to him. But even so, if you even met him once, he would have made you feel like you were something special.

Oh, Chad, I don't want to go back to my seat. I don't want to have this be done. I don't want to have the finality of this funeral. I don't want people to forget you, or not remember your smile or your laugh or your dumb jokes or the nicknames you gave everybody. I don't want to do this. I don't want to leave you alone and I don't want to miss you every single day. But I will. I will because it's what you expected of me and what you asked me to do.

The world lost a great man last Friday, and I am sorry to all the people who will never get a chance to be affected by your presence. But, thank you for being in my world and walking this life with me. I will never, ever, ever, forget who you were, and I will never stop telling anybody who will listen.

You fought the good fight. You were a warrior both at work and at home and you inspired me and so many people. You never complained, and you never wanted anybody to worry about you. You were admirable. You were so good. You were so, so good. I miss you, and I always will.

About the Author

Diana Register is a California transplant living in the beautiful state of Idaho. As a new widow, she is leaning how to embrace her grief and find her "grief gifts" in the new life she is learning how to navigate. With the help of her friends, family and amazing children, Stephen, Savanna, Shane and Kaitlyn, she is not just learning how to survive, but how to flourish and thrive in her grief. It is her greatest wish that she can help others who are grieving find their paths as well. Diana also founded the IAM149 foundation in her late husband's honor that gives back to pancreatic cancer patients (www.iam149.org). Check her out on Facebook (Grief Life) and watch for Grief Life to hit the road when she begins grief seminars. You can also find her writing on www.lovewhatmatters.com and on Facebook at Diana Stefano Register - Author.

87407060R00168

Made in the USA
San Bernardino, CA
04 September 2018